A GUIDE TO
TUNING MUSICAL INSTRUMENTS

JOHN MEFFEN

DAVID & CHARLES
Newton Abbot   London   North Pomfret (Vt)

To Kathleen, Sarah and Elizabeth

British Library Cataloguing in Publication Data
Meffen, John
  A guide to tuning musical instruments.
  1. Musical instruments
  2. Tuning
  I. Title
  781.91   MT165

ISBN 0-7153-8169-5

©John Meffen 1982

All rights reserved. No part of this
publication may be reproduced, stored
in a retrieval system, or transmitted,
in any form or by any means, electronic,
mechanical, photocopying, recording or
otherwise, without the prior permission
of David & Charles (Publishers) Limited

Typeset by Typesetters (Birmingham) Ltd.,
Smethwick, Warley, West Midlands
and printed in Great Britain
by Biddles Limited, Guildford, Surrey
for David & Charles (Publishers) Limited
Brunel House   Newton Abbot   Devon

Published in the United States of America
by David & Charles Inc
North Pomfret   Vermont 05053   USA

CONTENTS

1 What is tuning?   5
2 Why temper anyway?   16
3 How to temper   34
4 Tuning keyboard instruments   64
5 Brass and woodwind instruments   91
6 Stringed instruments   109
7 Percussion instruments   129
8 A guide to the history of temperament   132

Appendices
   1: Schemes for setting a variety of keyboard temperaments   144
   2: The cent value of a variety of intervals within an octave 154
   Glossary   155
   Bibliography   156
   Index   159

PREFACE

A study of tuning and temperament, lying, as it does somewhere between science and music, touches on many specialist areas. It has been my good fortune during the preparation of this book and my research into keyboard temperament which preceded it, to have had advice and assistance from many friends who are experts in their own fields. My indebtedness to Dr Richard Smith and Dave James of Boosey & Hawkes has already been acknowledged in the text, but I would like here to mention others whose names do not appear, but without whose help the book would have been the poorer.

No study of this nature can be undertaken without books, and I would like to thank Mrs Charlesworth and her staff at the Darlington Public Library for all the help they have given me in procuring books.

My initial research into temperament was guided, first, by Dr Jerome Roche of Durham University, and later by my friend Frank Mumby of Leeds University who asked the right questions and gave generously of his extensive knowledge of keyboard music, instruments and, though he often denied it, temperament.

It was Professor Sir James Beament who first encouraged me to think that I had information worthy of publication. Somehow, in his busy life as Head of the Department of Applied Biology at Cambridge, he has always managed to find time to reply at length to my letters, and has given invaluable advice on details of the intricacies of tuning as well as supplying the information on the number of notes audible within an octave at different pitch levels.

Thanks too, to my friends Layton Ring, who first got me started on harpsichord tuning and gave me much of the information on tuning viols, and Dennis Woolley, who made my harpsichord and allowed me to use the picture on p86. Mr John Arran was most helpful in clarifying ideas on guitar tuning, and Mrs Sylvia Pursey gave me valuable advice about the layout of the figures on p40 but any mistakes in calculation are of my own making.

My thanks too, to my wife, Kathleen, who could still find it in her heart after being sorely neglected in favour of a typewriter, to draw the excellent diagrams for me.

Finally, I am very grateful to my friend and colleague J. Victor Pollard who, when he himself was very busy, read all the initial drafts and made numerous helpful suggestions.

1
WHAT IS TUNING?

The answer to the question, 'What is tuning?' may appear to be so self-evident that the question itself is superfluous. One just tunes, what possible question could there be? But persisting with the question could be embarrassing. Many who play musical instruments which are tuned by the player may know the names of the notes to which the instrument should be tuned, and have at least some idea of setting those notes correctly, but would be unable to give an account of the principles of tuning. The tuning notes will have been learned along with basic technique, and it may also have been suggested that it is better to tune by playing two notes at once as a check for accuracy, but a direct question about what to listen for when tuning may not elicit as clear and direct an answer. There is a certain mystique which surrounds being in tune, both in the initial tuning process and in playing, which performers discuss in veiled terms, but about which very few are willing to be precise.

Reluctance to be drawn into making a pronouncement about tuning is understandable. Being in tune is crucial to music making, but giving a clear definition of it is not always easy. Describing the tuning process for a particular instrument may not be too difficult, but giving a precise account of being in tune in performance is much more difficult. It is usually assumed that one has, or has not, the ear for it, as one has the eye for drawing or painting or the palate for wine.

One reason why it is easier to be precise about tuning an instrument than about being in tune is that the former is static, involving, in some cases, only very few notes, while the latter changes from moment to moment as the music unfolds. Yet even the static tuning, although it can be precisely determined, is not always simple to understand. For instance, if a violinist and a guitarist are going to play together, they will select a common note from which to tune and then begin to tune their respective instruments. But is the process the same in each case? The short answer is no. The physical tightening and loosening of strings, and the checking of intervals, may to the uninitiated appear to be the same. Leaving aside for the moment the fact that the guitar has more strings than the violin, and therefore must be tuned to different notes, the musical aspect of the tuning will differ; because the players will be listening for different things while they are tuning, they will produce two different types of tuning despite having started from the same note. Having tuned, each in his own way, correctly but differently, how can they then play in tune with each other? And what is meant by playing in tune anyway, if they are in tune for one note only, in the tuning process itself?

The notions expressed in the preceding paragraph are confusing enough, but the next obvious question must be, if two artists have tuned their instruments correctly but differently, can the word 'tune' be appropriate in each case if the notes produced by the tuning process are different? Surely one instrument must be in tune, and the other out of tune. Furthermore, if one of them is out of tune, it must deliberately have been put out of tune, so why bother to take time to deliberately 'out-of-tune it', if such a combination of words is allowable?

It must surely be apparent that there are questions to be asked and answered, so perhaps a dictionary, musical or otherwise, may assist. Here, the information is generally given in two ways. The first is to give a definition only of tuning. Most dictionaries beg the question by defining 'to tune' as 'to put in tune' or 'to put (violin, piano, etc) in tune'. They do, however, mention other uses of the word 'tune'; to 'tune in' a radio means 'to adjust it to the right wavelength', or to 'tune' an internal combustion engine means 'to adjust it so as to make it work more smoothly and efficiently'. The word 'adjust' appears also in the definitions given in musical dictionaries (eg 'adjustment of strings . . . or pipes . . . to their proper pitch', or 'the adjustment to a recognised scale of any musical instrument'). The word adjust in each of these definitions is used in the physical sense of manipulating apparatus forming part of the instrument itself. *The Oxford Companion to Music* gives the meaning of tune as 'to bring into correct intonation' but then leads into the second way in which information on tuning is given, by directing the reader, under the heading 'Tuning of Instruments', to 'see Temperament'. It is by reference to temperament that the second source of information on tuning comes.

In looking up definitions of temperament, the word 'adjust'

again appears. Continuing with *The Oxford Companion to Music*, temperament means, 'an adjustment in tuning in order to get rid of gross inaccuracies in the intervals between certain notes'. This type of adjustment seems highly desirable! The *Concise Oxford Dictionary* gives a more gently worded definition; 'adjustment of intervals in tuning of piano etc so as to fit the scale for use in all keys', while the *Harvard Dictionary of Music* goes into more detail by defining it as 'a system of tuning in which the intervals deviate from the "pure" (acoustically correct) intervals of the Pythagorean system and just intonation'. There are obviously several leads to follow, since terms such as ' "pure" (acoustically correct) intervals', 'Pythagorean system' and 'just intonation' are offered without qualification, but from these definitions it is clear that although the adjustment of something is required both in tuning and in tempering, different types of adjustment are intended in each case. In tempering it is no longer the simple manipulation of the apparatus which is being described, but the adjustments of relationships between musical intervals, a much more complex process. The definitions do not give any indication of the type or size of these adjustments, nor do they offer any guiding principles for ascertaining them. Perhaps it is not reasonable to expect any meaningful discussion of such matters in a definition, but to anyone who wishes to tune an instrument, they are vital.

Tuning versus tempering
One fact emerges immediately from this search for definitions; the words tuning and tempering are not synonymous. They are, however, closely linked. Tuning may, or may not, involve tempering, but tempering always involves tuning. For convenience, the word tuning is used to cover both operations, and the essential difference between each process can become obscured. The word tune can have two separate though closely allied meanings. The first of these refers to the manipulation of the apparatus of a particular instrument in order to make it playable, without specifying the musical elements involved. The second refers to rendering an instrument playable by setting intervals which are pure or just (words which will require explanation). To temper, however, means to render an instrument playable by setting intervals which are not pure or just.

A further reference to the two instruments previously mentioned may help to clarify the position. A violin is tuned. That is the correct and only term to use, because the apparatus of the instrument is manipulated in such a way that the intervals between adjacent strings are pure. The definition of tuning is here satisfied in both instances. When referring to the guitar, the word tuning applies only to the manipulation of the pegs, because the intervals between adjacent strings, when correctly set, are not pure but are adjusted to some other pre-determined relationship with each other; the intervals between them are tempered.

It would seem that a clearer and more accurate description of what is actually happening could be given if the word tune were to be used only when the intervals involved were pure, and the word temper used when they were not. In this instance, a violin would still be tuned, but a guitar would be tempered. The likelihood of such an alteration in terminology catching on is very remote and not, in fact, entirely justifiable on every occasion. 'Tempering up' does not roll so readily off the tongue as 'tuning up' (although it may do with use), even though in certain circumstances it could be more accurate. To make this sort of distinction between tuning and tempering would necessitate the alteration of many other time-honoured phrases; to be in tune, or to be in temper, have, in general conversation, entirely different connotations.

In theory, it would be possible to distinguish between tuning and tempering when referring to any combinations of notes, but the complications produced by this apparent attempt at clarity might, in the end, confuse the situation even further. It is perhaps safer to keep to the present system of using the word tune indiscriminately and accepting without further qualification that with some instruments tempering is also needed. Doing so also implies a tacit acceptance that being in tune also means that tempering must, at times, take place.

To tune or not to tune
It may seem to be a simple matter to list those instruments which are tuned and those which are also tempered, and to some extent it is. There are two main guides in making a decision. The first is, if a player actually makes each separate note (ie has the opportunity to make a note slightly sharp or flat at will), the instrument in question needs only to be tuned. The second is, if a player can only select notes which have previously been determined, then the instrument in question must be tempered.

With only two guides, it would appear that there are only two categories. This is not strictly true, but some instruments can be classified immediately. The violin, and other members of the same family (viola, violoncello and, depending on how it is viewed, the double bass) are capable of producing any alteration in pitch the player may wish, no matter how small it may be. These instruments are in no way governed by the system which divides an octave into twelve semitones, although they can conform to this system if required to do so. All the members of this instrumental family need only be tuned; any tempering which may be needed to allow them to play in tune with other instruments can be done at the moment of performing.

Fretted instruments (guitars, viols, etc) are, by their construction, virtually confined to a scale of twelve semitones to the octave. In the hands of a skilled player, controlled variations in pitch are possible within limits. These instruments, therefore, come into the category of instruments which need to be tempered as well as tuned. The performer is also usually the tuner, and accurate tuning of these instruments demands knowledge and experience. The exact extent to which the intervals are tempered during the process of tuning is governed by the frets and therefore conforms to standard practice, but tempering the intervals during performance is a matter of judgement and discrimination.

Keyboard instruments, like those with frets, have visible demarcations of notes. The exact pitch of each note is decided by the tuner, and the player can only select but has no power to alter them. A slight anomaly exists in the case of the clavichord, on which instrument the player can vary the pitch of a note. This is, however, a special effect, particular only to this keyboard instrument. It does not materially affect the general intonation of the instrument (although it does make it somewhat more difficult to tune), but in performance, the player must beware of striking the key too strongly, thereby raising the pitch of the note. The standard keyboard gives twelve different keys within an octave and this obvious limitation of notes is a clear indication that tempering is required. The keys imply that C sharp = D flat, D sharp = E flat and so on, but in fact these notes are not equivalents. In certain tuning systems C sharp will be flatter than D flat, but in others it will be sharper. Only in equal temperament are these notes the exact equivalent of each other. The complications arising from keyboards and their need of tempering have provoked much argument over the centuries, arguments which show little sign of abating. The tyranny of the keyboard is felt by many musicians, but the restriction imposed by the use of only one temperament, which is comparatively recent, grew with the rise of the piano to pre-eminence in the nineteenth century. Other types of keyboard tempering are available, but they must all suffer from the same deficiency, that of being static.

There is one further category which includes all those instruments which are tempered by nature of their design and during their manufacture. All instruments with finger holes, valves or keys used for governing pitch, fall into this category. Taking a simple instrument like a recorder as an example, there are no keys on most recorders and the range is in the region of two octaves, give or take a few notes, depending on the pitch of the instrument and its quality and design (as well as the ability of the player). There are standard holds, or fingerings, for each note of the scale, and provided the breath pressure is carefully controlled, these holds will produce an equally tempered chromatic scale within each octave. The instrument does so because the holes are bored in such a way that vibrating lengths of the column of air within it will produce these notes. Theoretically, if any one of its notes is brought into tune with the corresponding note on another instrument, the rest of the instrument will automatically be brought into correct tune. This is done by making small adjustments to the position of the head joint of the recorder. In practice, however, this is true only within limits, because there are other factors which allow for only a small variation in the pitch of the tuning note.

Instruments with valves behave in a similar fashion, although there are differences. Valves have the effect of incorporating additional lengths of tubing into the system of the instrument, each additional length being designed to alter the pitch by a semitone or multiples of semitones. The size of a semitone can vary, but it is generally held to be half an equally tempered tone, or the distance between any two adjacent notes on a keyboard. This immediately implies that the instrument is tempered, and since the additional lengths of tubing are part of the instrument itself, then the instrument must be tempered both by its design and during its manufacture. One exception among brass instruments is the slide trombone. Since the player has absolute control over how far the slide can move, enabling fractional alterations in pitch to be made at will in much the same way as a violinist can alter notes by movement along the finger board, the trombone is not tempered during manufacture, but it can conform to a tempered scale if necessary.

To sum up on the question 'to tune or not to tune', instruments fall into three categories, namely, those which are free to make any note they wish within their compass, those which by the nature of their keys (or, in the case of the harp, its individually tuned strings) cannot make fractional alterations of pitch during performance, and finally those which are governed by finger holes, frets or valves, but have a small amount of latitude to vary pitch during performance. These classifications are by no means new. Hercole Bottrigari writing in 1594 (a treatise called *Il Desiderio*) described instruments as follows:

> The stable instruments are those which after they have been tuned by a conscientious Maestro, cannot be altered by any means. Such are Organs, Harpsichords, Spinets, Double Harps, and other similar instruments, which can produce only the pure diatonic scale which pleases most people or seems to please them. The stable but alterable instruments are all those which after they have been tuned by a diligent player, can be changed, augmented or diminished in some degree, according to the good judgement of the player as he touches their frets a little higher or lower. This occurs with the Lute and Viol, even though they have the stability of their frets. The same thing happens with the wind instruments such as straight and transverse Flutes and straight and curved Cornetts. Even though they have a certain stablility because of their holes, the accomplished player can nonetheless use a little less or a little more breath and can open the vents a little more or a little less, bringing them closer to a good accord. Expert players do this. The instruments which are completely alterable are those which have neither fingerboards nor holes — Trombones, Ribechini, Lire and the like. These having ordinarily neither frets nor openings can wander here and there according to the will of the player, and can be limited by lengthening or shortening of the "draws" (as the tubes of the Trombone are called) or by loosening or tightening of the lips. And likewise with the Lira and Ribechini the note can be altered by touching the strings over the neck either higher or lower, at the will and pleasure of the player.

Although the names of some of the instruments in the above quotation may now be strange, their types can be easily recognised. However, Bottrigari goes on to make a statement completely at variance with modern music making:

There remains to speak of the combining of all these species of instruments — stable as well as stable-alterable and entirely alterable. But since I told you that this cannot be done except with the greatest disunion, such as you heard today and described to me, I would advise you never to make such an orchestra, for it can only be done with the greatest difficulty, and is next to impossible.

So much for our favourite piano concerto at the Proms, a type of work which requires instruments from all groups. Bottrigari is here trying to explain why his questioner, when he thought he 'would hear a celestial harmony' instead 'heard confusion rather than the contrary, accompanied by a discordance'. Musical fashions have changed considerably since 1594, not least in our acceptance of a grouping of instruments which Bottrigari did not like. What he is discussing here in *Il Desiderio* is intonation, a topic still generating heat in discussion today.

Pitch

The term pitch, like tune, is used in many different but closely allied ways. It most usually appears in phrases such as high pitch or low pitch, in reference to voices or instruments, as well as to transpositions of song accompaniments. The term 'Concert Pitch' still persists too, particularly in the brass, wind and military band worlds. According to *The Oxford Companion to Music*:

> The vague expression 'Concert Pitch' may require some elucidation. English dictionaries define it as 'slightly higher than the ordinary' (*Oxford Concise Dictionary*), 'rather higher than usual' (Professor H. C. Wyld's *Universal Dictionary of the English Language*). . . .
> Probably the distinction implied is between the ordinary domestic piano, possibly old and low in pitch, and a piano intended for public use . . . The expression 'Concert Pitch', then, if interpreted exactly means 'A = 440' and if interpreted loosely means merely 'high in pitch'.

A wind player, using the term 'C Concert', has simply dropped the word pitch, and is referring to the note C on a piano as distinct from the C on his instrument.

Pitch is relative. It is related either to some other instruments or voices, or to a specific frequency. To say that something is high or low pitched does not necessarily specify how high or how low, but to refer to a specific frequency, does. Standard pitch is now usually accepted as $a' = 440$ Hertz (the note A above middle

C on a piano is produced by a frequency of 440 vibrations per second). The pitch of every other note in the scale can be calculated exactly from this information (whatever the scale might be), but it is usual to specify, in general descriptions, the vibration rate of a', c' or c''. At a' 440 Hertz, c' is 261.62 Hertz, and c'' is 523.24 Hertz.

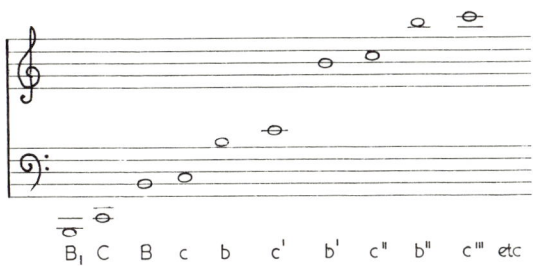

Explanation of the letters used for signifying pitch throughout the book

This pitch standard was adopted at an international conference held in London under the auspices of the International Standards Association in 1939, and replaced the old standard a' 435 Hertz, which had been fixed by the Paris Academy in 1859 and confirmed at a conference in Vienna in 1865. Although a' 440 Hertz still remains the standard, there is a tendency, for concert purposes, to raise the pitch above this level, while for performances of early music, particularly those given on authentic or replica instruments, the pitch often used is a' 415 Hertz, a semitone lower than a' 440 Hertz.

While in theory at least, and usually in practice too, it is possible to alter the pitch of stringed instruments, it must be remembered that instruments, like people, become accustomed to certain types of treatment, and can be upset by change. For instance, a harpsichord, generally tuned to ¼-comma meantone will tend to revert to its own version of that temperament after it has been altered to equal temperament. Unfortunately an instrument will not uniformly change back to its old form of tuning, it does so in patches, making the general sound most unpleasant.

In some cases, a change of pitch is impossible. A high-pitched woodwind instrument cannot be brought down to standard pitch. Some latitude is available on certain wind instruments to allow for tuning, but unless the instrument is specifically designed for it, the limit of pitch alteration is very narrow. On other instruments the pitch can be changed, but at a price. Many high-pitched pipe organs have been brought down to standard pitch. A complete renovation is required and new pipes are usually necessary for at least the lowest notes in each tone colour. Similarly, harmoniums can be brought down to standard pitch, but not without time and expense.

Being in tune

From such a hodge-podge of instruments – some stable, some stable but alterable and some entirely alterable in intonation, and each tuned in its own particular way – is it possible to say what is or is not in tune? The answer to that question must be, yes, because most people, trained musicians or not, cringe when something is out of tune. It is the negative aspect of being out of tune which is most generally obvious; the more positive one of being in tune is less likely to attract attention, except from fellow musicians.

A keyboard player, unless also a tuner, can take no part in the search for being in tune. Intonation for every note on a keyboard is preordained, and the fixed tuning (or should it be tempering?) cannot fluctuate to the dictates of the music. For the intrumentalist who does not have this restriction, tuning is continuous; the set-piece pattern of tuning before performance begins is only part of the process. Tuning, in these circumstances, is live, and constantly changing. In theory every note played has to be separately tuned, and although experience and training make note finding almost automatic, the player must hear each note mentally before it is played in order to make any adjustments to it before it becomes audible to an audience. But it is by no means unknown for that adjustment to take place after the note has begun to sound!

During training, a musician is told to listen carefully and play in tune with others or with himself, but is seldom told precisely what to listen for. If he is able to play acceptably with experienced players, he is said to have 'a good ear', but little or no explanation is given as to what, exactly, needs to be done to acquire it. Although it is possible to say that something is not in tune, it is quite another matter to do something about it. A musician not only hears what should be played, but also feels, bodily, what action is necessary to achieve it. Both of these capacities can be improved by practice and guidance, but it is

WHAT IS TUNING?

obvious that some individuals start with great natural advantages. Most people can run, but very few will gain international recognition for doing so. This does not, however, stop them from using that skill, improving it and enjoying it. The same is true of music. There is some music in everyone which can be nurtured. An understanding of the physical facts involved, while it can never replace natural talent, can enhance whatever natural capabilities a person has.

2
WHY TEMPER ANYWAY?

At some point in a discussion of tuning and tempering, figures become necessary. It is often at this time that the musician withdraws. For some, the position is quite clear, mathematics has no place in their art, while others, fearing that the mathematical requirements will soon outstrip their knowledge, are reticent to take the first few steps. Perhaps the majority feel that mathematics, however interesting, has little bearing on workaday problems. It may be all right for theorists, but is of little real value to practitioners. Each of these arguments may hold at least a grain of truth, but hardly justify dismissing the subject without giving it reasonable consideration. It is obvious that no amount of calculation can make someone who is devoid of musical ability play well and in tune. It is equally obvious, however, that a knowledge of what to listen for when deciding whether or not an interval is acoustically correct, is of considerable value. Such knowledge also creates an acceptable working vocabulary for the discussion of tuning. If musicians were taught to listen to the constitution of the notes they play, it would be helpful in isolating the pitch at which discrepancies occur to cause a note to sound out of tune, and so increase awareness of what exactly was wrong, as well as the ability to rectify it both in tuning and in the wider context of being in tune.

The mathematics required to gain a working knowledge of tuning and tempering is small. The four rules of addition, subtraction, multiplication and division are sufficient in most instances, but a knowledge of logarithms, as well as the ability to use a calculator, will speed matters if you wish to work out all the basic calculations. For those who find this prospect daunting, it is possible to tune accurately and understand what is happening without the need of calculation at all. Most of the figures used from time to time are for guidance and comparison, and are, therefore, easily understandable; only those who wish need delve deeper into mathematical mysteries.

Musical sound is caused by periodic vibrations, produced

either consecutively or concurrently (or both) by a variety of media. For a musician, the media are instruments, and the vibrations they produce, depending on their speeds, form the notes we hear. In order to make recognisable melodies and harmonies, the notes occur at various pitches within the limited capacity of human hearing, and it is the intervals between these pitches, combined with their rhythmic pattern, that is recognised as music. A series of musical intervals produced consecutively and with a particular rhythmic pattern constitutes a melody, while musical intervals struck concurrently constitute harmony. Western music is based on scales made up of twelve semitones, corresponding approximately to the black and white keys on a piano contained within any octave. The reason for including the word approximately will be apparent later, but the general division of a scale into twelve more or less equal semitones is a sufficiently good starting point. Such a succession of semitones is known as the *chromatic* scale, but this is reduced to a *diatonic* scale of eight notes (less in the case of *whole tone* and *pentatonic* scales). The eight note scales are the major and minor scales in common use, and the intervals used in music are described in relation to these scales. The interval formed by notes one and two of the scale is called a second, that formed by notes one and three is a third, and so on. In a major scale the intervals of a 2nd, 3rd, 6th and 7th are called major, and the 4th, 5th and octave are called perfect. If a major interval is made narrower by a semitone, without altering the letter names of the two notes concerned, it is then called minor. For example, C to E is a major third, but C sharp to E and C to E flat are both minor thirds. Similarly, if a minor interval is made wider by a semitone without altering the letter names of either note, it becomes major. Again without altering the letter name of either note, if a major or a perfect interval is widened by a semitone it is called augmented, while a minor or a perfect interval made narrower by a semitone is called diminished. For example, D to A is a perfect fifth, but D flat to A, or D to A sharp are augmented fifths. Similarly, F to D flat is a minor sixth, but F sharp to D flat is a diminished sixth. Should anyone be in doubt about the quality or size of intervals (particularly major, minor and perfect), it would be safer to have a book of the rudiments of music available to consult.

The harmonic series

Music is composed of intervals, but it is unfortunate that if they are tuned true they will not fit together within the confines of a scale. Taking first the intervals which form the common chord, namely the intervals of a major third, a perfect fifth and an octave, L. S. Lloyd, in his book *Intervals, Scales and Temperaments* writes: 'If we tune upwards from any given note in a series of octaves, perfect fifths or true major thirds we never reach a unison again between the notes of any two of the series however far we go.' A glance at a piano keyboard seems to belie this statement. Perhaps the most obvious instance in which two of these series appear to fit happily together is in the relationship between major thirds and an octave. Starting at middle C (c') on a piano, three consecutive major thirds fit exactly into an octave $c' - c''$. Yet L. S. Lloyd states that this is not possible. To make any headway, the physical facts about the nature of sounds need to be considered. So far as temperament is concerned, these are based primarily on the harmonic series, the first fifteen notes of which appear below as Example 1.

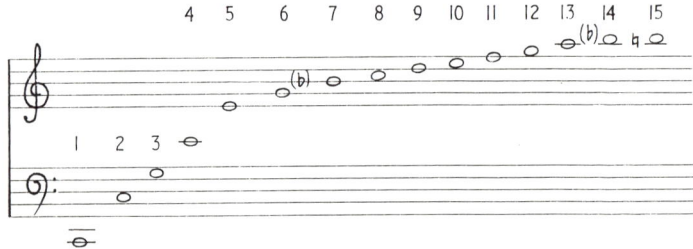

Example 1 The first fifteen notes of the harmonic series beginning on note C.

This series contains some of the notes which can be formed from a length of string or column of wind capable of producing the lowest note. The second note in the series is formed by half the length of string, the third note by ⅓ of the length of string, the fourth by ¼ of the length of string and so on. Each of these notes is called a harmonic; the lowest is the fundamental or first harmonic, its octave is the second harmonic, its twelfth is the third harmonic and its double octave the fourth harmonic. Theoretically the series could continue indefinitely, but in practice it is limited by the elasticity of the vibrating material and by the limitations of human hearing.

WHY TEMPER ANYWAY? 19

It is from information supplied by the harmonic series that minor excursions into the realms of mathematics will be made. The series shows that the ratio between a note and its octave is as 2:1, and between a note and its major third the ratio is as 5:4 (c' - e' being the first major third in the above series). If three major thirds equal one octave, then $5/4 \times 5/4 \times 5/4$ should equal $2/1$, which it obviously does not. In fact $5/4 \times 5/4 \times 5/4 = {}^{125}/_{64}$, which is short of 2:1 by ${}^{125}/_{128}$. This fraction represents the interval by which three major thirds, if tuned true, fall short of an octave; an interval with the ratio of 125:128. Although ratios are, in most cases, adequate for the measurement of musical intervals, they soon become cumbersome and eventually, with some forms of tempering, unsuitable. A much simpler method of measurement to understand is that devised by A. J. Ellis, the translator of *On the Sensations of Tone* by Helmholtz. This method is based on a system of cent values, each semitone on a piano keyboard (ie each semitone in an equally tempered scale) representing 100 cents, making an octave of 1200 cents. There is a list of cent values for various notes of the scale, in the appendix, together with information on the calculation of cent values for anyone who wishes to be self-sufficient, but the cent values for the intervals which are of immediate interest are as follows:

	True	In Equal Temperament
Major 3rd	386 cents	400 cents
Perfect 5th	702 cents	700 cents
Perfect 4th	498 cents	500 cents
Octave	1200 cents	1200 cents

Looking again at the three major thirds which ostensibly form an octave:

$$\text{an octave} = 1200 \text{ cents}$$
$$\text{three major thirds} = 3 \times 386 = 1158 \text{ cents}$$
$$\text{Difference} = 42 \text{ cents}$$

This difference is considerable; almost half a semitone. Without having the facility to tune three major thirds and check the resultant note against an octave, the interval of half a semitone (not available on the normal keyboard) may seem negligible, but a discrepancy of this magnitude is easily audible. Experiments have shown that in the octave at the bottom of the piano keyboard it is possible to distinguish approximately nineteen different pitches. These pitches must be about 63 cents apart. In the octave around middle C (c'), this number has jumped to fifty in an octave, making intervals of 24 cents audible, while in the highest octave of the piano a staggering 350 different pitches are discernible, making a movement of less than 3.5 cents noticeable. Compared with this information, a movement of 42 cents is large in all but the lowest octaves of the piano. These figures are for noticeable movements, not comparisons, in pitch. If two notes which are not quite in tune with each other are struck simultaneously, another phenomenon, called beating, becomes evident. Since beating takes place, except for the octave itself, at least an octave above the higher of the two notes simultaneously struck (and in many cases more than an octave), this immediately brings the pitches at which dissonance occurs into the higher, and therefore more easily discernible, octaves. Beating and its importance in tuning will be discussed later; reference has been made to it here solely to dispel any doubts a reader may have of his ability to hear an interval of 42 cents.

Returning to the difficulties with major thirds, which on a keyboard, appear to make up an octave, the notation makes it clear, too, that something is wrong. An enharmonic change (a change of note name, but not, on a keyboard, a change of pitch, eg D sharp for E flat), is required if three thirds are to fit exactly into an octave. Starting from middle C (c'), $c' - e'$ is a major third, $e' - g'$ sharp is a major third, but g' sharp $- c''$ is a diminished fourth, the name of g' sharp has to be changed to a' flat to make the interval into a major third. This may seem to be a carping distinction to make when everyone knows that on a modern keyboard g' sharp $= a'$ flat, but this equality applies only to a *modern* keyboard. The method of tuning which produces this situation only became established in England in the middle of the nineteenth century and was still a source of irritation to many musicians at the end of that century. What does show up clearly from this simple calculation is that G sharp is 42 cents lower than A flat when these two notes are arrived at in pure thirds from C; similarly any enharmonic equivalents (F sharp and G flat, D sharp and E flat, etc) would be 42 cents at variance with each other if the same tuning methods were applied.

Unfortunately these are not the only discrepancies which occur when attempts are made to tune in pure intervals. Referring again to a keyboard and using only major thirds, perfect fifths and octaves, the following equations should be correct:

WHY TEMPER ANYWAY? 21

12 perfect 5ths = 7 octaves
4 perfect 5ths = 2 octaves + a major 3rd
8 perfect 5ths + a major 3rd = 5 octaves

It must be obvious by now that they will not, but by how much are they awry?

```
12 perfect 5ths    = 12 × 702      = 8424
7 octaves          =  7 × 1200     = 8400
                   Difference        24 cents
```

This is an important discrepancy known as the comma of Pythagoras, or the ditonic comma.

```
4 perfect 5ths         = 4 × 702           = 2808
2 octaves + a major 3rd = (2 × 1200) + 386 = 2786
                       Difference             22 cents
```

This again is an important discrepancy which is known as the comma of Didymus, or more usually, the syntonic comma.

```
8 perfect 5ths + a major 3rd = (8 × 702) + 386 = 6002
5 octaves                    = 5 × 1200        = 6000
                             Difference            2 cents
```

This small discrepancy is known as a schisma.

Finally, to keep matters right, the original calculation for three major 3rds and an octave should also be included.

```
1 octave      = 1 × 1200   = 1200
3 major 3rds  = 3 × 386    = 1158
              Difference      42 cents
```

This discrepancy is known as a diesis.

In the performance of music these discrepancies must be eliminated or accommodated and this is the process known as tempering. All music must be tempered if it is to fit into the usual pattern of scales. Human voices and instruments which have the freedom to alter pitch at will (the entirely alterable instruments of Chapter 1), can have a fully flexible scale, and those instruments which can alter their pitch within closely controlled limits (all the stable but alterable instruments of Chapter 1), have, to some extent, a flexible scale. On these instruments it is possible to accommodate the discrepancies in the most desirable way at the moment of performance. On stable instruments, however, the scale to be used is frozen into solid form in the act of tuning, and no amount of thawing is possible during performance. So the keyboard scale is rigid, and consequently a compromise between the desirable and the tolerable. The conclusion was drawn in the first chapter that tuning means either the manipulation of an instrument to make it playable or making that instrument playable by setting pure or just intervals on it, and that tempering means rendering an instrument playable by setting intervals which are not pure or just. Tempering is the fixing of intervals during tuning or performing which will give the best compromise for the instrument and the music concerned. In the last paragraph that compromise was described as being between the desirable and the tolerable. It could be assumed that the desirable would always be pure intervals and the compromise always be tempered ones, but this assumption is not correct in all cases. As usual, a decision cannot be arrived at in quite such simple terms. The judgement, as in life generally, is seldom between black and white, but, more often, between various shades of grey. In this case, white would be pure intervals, but black would not be all impure intervals, even though, by definition, that which is not pure must, in some degree, be impure. A more accurate definition of black would have to be intolerably impure intervals, even though, paradoxically, the more accurate the definition, the less precise it seems to be. For the moment, at least, it is the best which can be given. This leaves the main working area as the grey one which includes all degrees of impurity between the pure and the intolerable.

Listening for and recognising harmonics
Since the intolerable is difficult to define precisely, it is better to begin with the pure. All tuning schemes are based on the manipulation of thirds, fourths and fifths within pure octaves, so some definition of purity, at least in regard to these intervals, needs to be established. To be able to recognise purity, it is necessary to understand the phenomenon known as beating. Beating is an upleasant sensation felt when two notes not quite in tune with each other are sounded together. The sensation is a 'wowing' or 'yawing' sound, which, depending on its speed, can range from soothing, through exciting, to very unpleasant. Roger North, the eighteenth-century writer on various musical matters, puts it very nicely:

WHY TEMPER ANYWAY?

This is to help a learner to find out the way to come at the accord he aimes at; but the justice of it, according to purest harmony, is more nice, and requires other sort of observation; and that is of the chattering, wallowing, or rowling of two tones sounding together, which will be very notable, till the accord is exact, and then a perfect tranquillity takes place, without any such dissention.

As the notes concerned are moved further apart, the distance becomes recognisable as a new interval and therefore acceptable. If the distance between them is further increased, there will be areas, however far apart the notes are produced, when it is again betwixt and between acceptable intervals, and beating will once more be noticeable. Beating is caused by some of the harmonics of the notes concerned being slightly at variance with each other when they ought, in fact, to be coinciding exactly.

The sensation of beating can be felt without its exact cause being understood or located. For an instrumental tuner, the understanding and location of beats is a skill which must be acquired. Since beating is caused when harmonics which should coincide exactly do not do so, the first step in acquiring this skill is to be able to isolate the pitches at which the relevant harmonics from any given note occur.

Example 1 shows the harmonic series beginning on C. When a note is played on almost any instrument, other notes of its harmonic series will be audible. It depends on the instrument which notes in the series can be heard; some instruments such as the flute, have few harmonics, while electrically produced notes have none at all, although on many instruments using electrically produced notes some harmonics are added to give 'colour' to the sound. But on most instruments, as well as the first, the second, third, fourth and fifth harmonics are easy to hear, and many higher harmonics are also audible to anyone who has spent a little time learning how to listen for them. A piano is the easiest and most readily available instrument on which to experiment. Try playing the note c, an octave below middle C (c'), strike it firmly, hold the note down, and then listen carefully. As the note dies, middle C (c'), the G above it (g'), the C an octave above middle C (c'') and E above that (e''), should become audible. The notes tend to become audible in succession, so they will need time to build up. The further the harmonic is away from the struck note, the less strong (usually) it will be. The note e'' should be the weakest in the series so far, and will probably take the longest time to build up. For anyone who cannot hear these

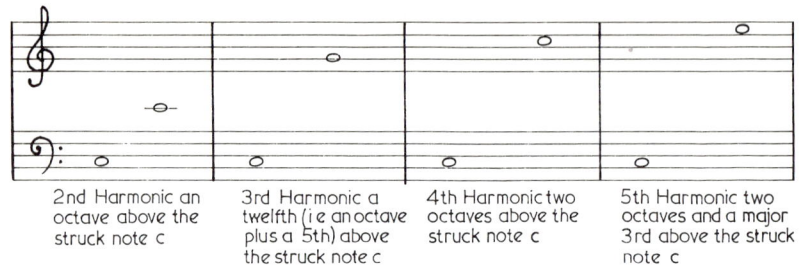

Example 2 The first five harmonics shown in relation to a bass note *c*

harmonics immediately, some training is necessary.

The training process is simple. Before striking the note *c* again, lightly touch middle C (*c'*) and memorise its pitch. Now strike *c* again, and, holding the note down, listen carefully. It will take a second or two for the jangle of the struck string to die down, but when the note is humming smoothly focus attention on the pitch middle C (*c'*), already memorised. The note will actually be so loud that it may easily be accepted as part of *c* itself rather than its octave. The note is so obvious that it sometimes takes a while to be convinced that it is not imagination. Having mastered the art of hearing the second harmonic of note *c*, try other notes in the same vicinity and listen for their second harmonic (it will always be an octave above the struck and held note). Some may be easier to hear than others, but keep on trying until it becomes automatic to focus attention on the second harmonic as well as on the first (or fundamental note). The higher the note, the less audible the harmonics.

Having learned how to recognise the second harmonic of any given note, return to note *c* and try to pick out the third harmonic, which is the note a twelfth above the original note (a brief check from Example 1 will allay any doubts about the pitch of the third harmonic). If any difficulty is experienced in hearing it, and here again it may be louder than expected, follow the same process which was suggested for the second harmonic by, on this occasion, gently striking the G above middle C (*g'*). After memorising the sound, strike *c* again, hold it down, and focus attention on the pitch *g'*. Having mastered the skill of listening for the third harmonic of note *c*, try listening for the third harmonic of other notes close to it, remembering that the third harmonic will always be the twelfth note above the one struck. Do not forget that in measuring musical intervals, count *both* the starting *and* the finishing notes.

Now try listening for the fourth harmonic above note c, which will be two octaves above the struck and held note. It is not necessary to describe the training process again, but the fourth harmonic may be quieter than the third, and will take a little longer to build up.

Having come to terms with recognising the fourth harmonic above note c and the notes immediately around it, carry on to the fifth harmonic. The process is the same as before, but it may take even longer for the note to build up. It will be fainter than the fourth harmonic, but persevere, it will be there! The fifth harmonic is the seventeenth note above the struck and held note, or, thinking of it a different way, it is two octaves and a major third above the struck and held note.

The skill acquired by listening for, and identifying the first five harmonics above a given note, is essential to even the most basic attempts at tuning a keyboard instrument. It is a useful, as well as entertaining, exercise in listening, to strike a note, hold it down, and then try to identify any other notes which build up from the original. On my own piano, for instance, for about an octave round note F (two octaves and a fifth below middle C or c'), the seventh and fifteenth harmonics are particularly clear, and from some notes the tenth harmonic is also strong. This type of discriminatory exercise is most useful, since knowing what to hear but ignore can be as helpful as knowing what to listen for. Harmonics which are audible but not immediately recognised can get in the way of positive listening. Once a harmonic has been classified, its usefulness (or otherwise) can be assessed.

Purity and beating

Returning to the discussion which occasioned this necessary digression on listening for harmonics, the question was, 'How are we to know when an interval is pure?' Beginning with an octave, by definition a true octave is formed between two notes when the second harmonic of the lower note coincides with the first harmonic of the upper. This is shown in musical notation in Example 3 below. The octave $c - c'$ will be exactly in tune if the first harmonic of c and the struck note c' agree perfectly. If, for the sake of argument, the upper note, (c') of the octave in Example 3 were to be made sharp by three vibrations per second, then the second harmonic of the lower note, also a c', could not coincide with it exactly. The actual frequencies would be as follows; the lower note, c, would have a frequency, if tuned to standard pitch, of 130.8 vibrations per second (130.8 Hertz), its second harmonic, c', would therefore be formed by twice that number of vibrations per second (261.62 Hertz). If the upper note of the octave, also a c', was giving out three vibrations per second more than 261.6 (ie 264.6 Hertz), the three extra vibrations per second would be heard as beats, or pulsations, in the sound, although the notes, in other respects, would appear to be the same. The slower the beat rate, the more difficult it is to hear it. For a rate of three beats per second, a metronome setting of 180 would give an accurate indication of the speed of the beating. If the upper note were to be gradually lowered in pitch, the beat rate would slow down, eventually stopping when the pitch of the note fell to 261.6 Herz. If the pitch of the upper note were to be lowered still further, and its frequency fell below 261.6 Herz, beating would start again. The $c - c'$ octave would be exactly in tune when there is no beating at pitch c'. Example 3 gives this information in staff notation.

Example 3 Showing the pitch at which the most audible beating takes place when tuning octaves and fifths. The harmonics are shown as guides (w) and those harmonics which should be in unison with each other are ringed

The fifth is similar to the octave to check for purity, except that the note to listen for when detecting beats (or the lack of them) is an octave above the upper note (or a twelfth above the lower), since, by definition, a perfect fifth is formed between two notes when the third harmonic of the lower note coincides with the second harmonic of the upper (see Example 3).

The examples below deal with perfect fourths and major thirds in a similar fashion. A perfect fourth occurs between two notes when the fourth harmonic of the lower note coincides with the third harmonic of the upper. The harmonics given in the first example show that the note to listen for when detecting the presence of beats is two octaves above the lower note.

A major third is formed between two notes when the fifth

Example 4 Showing the pitch at which the most audible beating takes place when tuning perfect fourths and major thirds. The harmonics are shown as guides (w), and those harmonics which should be in unison are ringed

harmonic of the lower note coincides with the fourth harmonic of the upper. At this distance from the fundamental, the harmonics are becoming less easy to discern, and there is the added complication that the fourth harmonic of the lower note is only a semitone away from the third harmonic of the upper, causing some dissonance. The effect of any interference can be overcome by listening intently for the correct harmonic, in this instance e'', focussing attention on that and resisting all temptations to accept the 'general' sound of the interval which is not so 'still' as a pure octave, fifth or fourth.

Difference tones and their use in tuning

Purity is recognisable, and the lack of it is measurable, at least so far as octaves, perfect fifths, perfect fourths and major thirds are concerned. It is recognisable in that harmonics can be heard to coincide, and the lack of it is measurable in that, if the harmonics do not coincide, the number of vibrations per second by which they are at variance with each other can be counted. It is also possible to establish whether that variation is on the sharp or on the flat side. But there are other ways of knowing when intervals and chords are in or out of tune, particularly if they are fairly high in pitch. Take, for instance, the triad of C major. Beginning on middle C, it will contain the notes $c' - e' - g'$. The frequency of c' will be 261.6 Hertz, and since for a major third the fifth harmonic of the lower note must coincide with the fourth harmonic of the upper, the ratio between the two frequencies must be as 4:5, the frequency of e' can be calculated as 261.6 Hertz × 5/4, which equals 327.0 Hertz. Similarly the frequency of g can be calculated as 261.6 Hertz × 3/2, which equals 392.4 Hertz. Each pair of these notes will form intervals, $c' - e'$ is a major third, $e' - g'$ is a minor third and $c' - g'$ is a perfect fifth. The vibrations causing these sounds, as well as

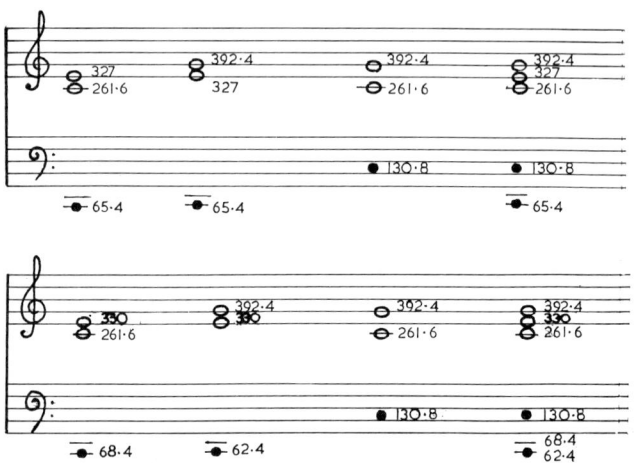

Example 5 Above, showing difference tones in a triad of c major when the notes are true. The struck notes are shown as semibreves and the difference tones as crotchets without tails. Below, showing difference tones in a triad of c major when the major third is raised by 3 Hertz from 327 Hertz to 330 Hertz. The two distinct pitches at low *c*, can be clearly heard

producing the intervals mentioned, will also produce difference tones, that is, notes resulting from the difference between the frequencies of each note in the interval. In the case of the major third, the new note produced will have a frequency 327.0 Hertz minus 261.6 Hertz, a frequency of 65.4 Hertz, which, since it is exactly a quarter of 261.6 Hertz, will be note C, two octaves below c'. The minor third $e' - g'$ will also give a difference tone which will have the frequency 392.4 Hertz minus 327.0 Hertz, again a frequency of 65.4 Hertz. If the two thirds $c' - e'$ and $e' - g'$ are exactly in tune, their difference tones should coincide at a pitch two octaves below c'. The difference tone formed by the fifth $c' - g'$ will have the frequency 392.4 Hertz minus 261.6 Hertz, which is 130.8 Hertz, exactly half of 261.6 Hertz, and producing a note *c*, an octave below c'. If the triad is exactly in tune, all of the notes, including those in the triad as well as the difference tones, will still be those which form the triad of C major. Let any of the original notes be wrong, and at least two of the difference tones must alter and become dissonant.

This is the cause of that elusive low note which seems to buzz about somewhere in mid air, when high-pitched instruments or voices are playing. Checking its accuracy for tuning purposes is intriguing. Three recorders playing the notes mentioned (remember that descant recorders sound an octave higher than the written pitch), or three female voices singing them, can demonstrate it immediately. If the instruments, or voices, are in tune, the difference tones remain steady and harmonise with each other and with the notes being played or sung. As an experiment, alter the pitch of the middle note, e', and listen to the lower difference tone. Instead of one, there will now be two, one higher than the low C and the other lower. Obviously, neither of these new difference tones will harmonise with the existing chord, with the result that an unpleasant buzzing sound, which appears to have no connection with anything else, is heard. The addition of a low-pitched instrument or voice has the immediate effect of lowering the difference tones to such a depth that they are difficult to hear as separate notes, as well as covering up the sound of the higher pitched difference tones which are still present.

Purity of intervals and chords is therefore something which can be demonstrated, measured, and, above all, clearly heard in various ways. What then of the intolerable, which is the opposite end of the spectrum? This is much more difficult and subjective, and could more appropriately be discussed as part of the history of temperament. Views on dissonance have changed from century to century, and will no doubt continue to change. These changes depend more on the compensations derived from greater flexibility, and the tolerance of composer and listener, than on the discussion of dissonance as a principle. Because of the physical impossibility of fitting pure thirds, fourths, fifths and octaves together within the framework of tonality, there have been fluctuations in the methods employed to make these intervals 'work' together in some acceptable fashion. On instruments with fixed scales, these methods have ranged from keeping the fifths and fourths as pure as possible, thus widening the thirds, to keeping the thirds as pure as possible and thereby narrowing the fifths and widening the fourths. These adjustments have usually been made within the confines of pure octaves, but there have been attempts to accommodate the discrepancies by altering the octaves. Such attempts are generally condemned by the writers who mention them. The present day compromise is equal temperament, which favours the fifths and fourths more than the thirds and keeps the octaves pure. It is equal only in that each key is equally in (or out of) tune, whereas the other forms of rigid scale give rise to some chords being better in tune than others. So far as instruments with flexible scales are concerned, arguments about the tolerable and the intolerable still continue every time musicians play together, but on instruments with rigid scales the tolerable and the intolerable are matters of fashion, and fashions change.

In attempting to answer the question, 'Why temper anyway?', certain digressions into peripheral areas have been necessary. The only true answer to the question is that we temper because we must; it is not an arbitrary matter, there is no alternative. It makes no difference that some forms of tempering are done subtly and others are not. If intervals are not true, they are tempered; there is no half way stage between the two. The only grey area is that of tolerability.

The pure scale

Before moving on to details of types of tempering, one further avenue needs exploration — that of scales. In *The Art of Music* Sir Hubert Parry reminds us that 'scales are made in the process of endeavouring to make music and continue to be altered and modified, generation after generation even till the art has arrived at a high degree of maturity'. Scales sum up current usage in melody and harmony. Although the number of scalic steps, so far as written music is concerned, is long established, the size of these steps is still a matter of debate. The rigidity of the scale set on a stable instrument applies to the so-called pure scale as well as to tempered scales. The reason can be easily shown. Starting from a note C, within an octave above it, a pure third, C – E, a pure fourth, C – F, and a pure fifth, C – G, could be tuned. Initially these intervals would give no trouble because their inversions, a minor sixth, E – C, a perfect fifth, F – C, and a perfect fourth, G – C, would also be pure intervals, and the minor third, E – G, incidentally produced in tuning these intervals, would also be pure. Difficulties would arise in establishing the other notes of the scale. By keeping a running picture of the scale, in cent values, as it builds, the difficulties become apparent. So far, the following notes will have been formed in relation to C, if they are all tuned pure:

C	E	F	G	C
0.	386	498	702	1200

From this it can be deduced that a semitone, E – F, will be 112 cents (the difference between 498 and 386), and that a whole tone, F – G, must be 204 cents. Since a major scale consists of tones and semitones, it should theoretically be easy to fit in the other notes. Note D should be 204 cents, a full tone above C, and likewise note E should be a full tone of 204 cents above D. Unfortunately the interval C – E is fixed as a pure third of 386 cents, and 386 minus 204 only leaves room for a tone of 182 cents between D and E. This produces two differently sized tones between C and E. Similar troubles occur higher up the scale between the notes G and C. The upper C is set at 1200 cents and the G at 702 cents, leaving 498 cents to be divided between the two tones and one semitone. Using the larger tone would mean that the distance between G and C would have to be 204 cents plus 204 cents plus 112 cents, making 520 cents which is too much, but using the lesser tone of 182 cents would mean 182 cents plus 182 cents plus 112 cents, making 476 cents, which is too little. These two figures each are a syntonic comma either above or below the 498 cents which exist between G and C. Accepting that the semitone B – C is 112 cents, the problem devolves on fitting two tones into 386 cents, just as it did between C and E originally. Using a similar solution, the difficulty arises as to which of the tones, G – A or A – B, should be 204 cents and which should be 182 cents. The scale being built in relation to C, note A should, perhaps, be a pure major sixth above C which would make it also a pure minor third below upper C. Since from the original pure intervals it was found that a pure minor third was formed between E and G, a distance of 316 cents, note A should be 884 cents (1200 cents minus 316 cents), making the tone G – A 182 cents (a lesser tone) and A – B 204 cents (a greater tone). The pure scale from C, in cent values, now looks like this:

```
    204         112   204              204        112
  ┌─────┐     ┌───┐ ┌────┐           ┌────┐    ┌────┐
  C     D       E    F     G           A        B       C
  0    204    386   498   702         884     1088    1200
       └──────────┘       └──────────┘
            182                 182
```

When looked at against the keyboard scale used today in which every semitone is 100 cents and every tone 200 cents, the differences are obvious:

```
  C    D    E    F    G    A    B    C
  0   200  400  500  700  900 1100 1200
```

32 WHY TEMPER ANYWAY?

Returning to the pure scale, it would be simple enough to tune the white notes of a keyboard to this scale, but since it has different sized tones, it can only 'work' starting on C. If it were to start on G, the first tone, G – A, would be wrong, and there would be similar difficulty with the key of D. The interval between the fifth and sixth degrees of the scales of G and D would also be the wrong size.

So far, only the white notes of the keyboard have been considered. Further complications arise when the black notes are admitted into the discussion. Still taking C as a starting point and dealing with thirds, fourths and fifths from existing notes, the next two notes to add to the scale would be E flat, a minor third above, and A flat a major third below, C, the new notes necessary for the scale of C minor. Making these two additions the pure scale will look like this:

C	D	E♭	E	F	G	A♭	A	B	C
0	204	316	386	498	702	814	884	1088	1200

This produces other semitones in the scale, D – E flat, E flat – E, G – A flat, and A flat – A. Their cent values must be as follows:

The D – E flat semitone is 316–204 cents = 112 cents
The E flat – E semitone is 386–316 cents = 70 cents
The G – A flat semitone is 814–702 cents = 112 cents
The A flat – A semitone is 884–814 cents = 70 cents

As well as the two sizes of tone discovered when dealing with the white notes, there are now two sizes of semitone, the diatonic semitone of 112 cents, and a new, chromatic, semitone of 70 cents. The two tones were found to be 22 cents, or a syntonic comma, different in size, while the two semitones differ by 42 cents, or a diesis.

The remaining three notes on a keyboard do not fit happily into the scale of C, but, depending on what they are called, their cent values could be calculated from the available information. If they were to be called C sharp, F sharp and B flat, their cent values would be 70, 568 and 1018 cents respectively, but if they were to be called D flat, G flat and A sharp, their cent values would be 134, 632 and 954 cents respectively. By adding these notes, yet another diatonic semitone, of 134 cents, is introduced. The cent values for these three notes were calculated as chromatic semitones from their respective natural notes; if, however, they were to be calculated as diatonic semitones, they would produce a new chromatic semitone of 92 cents. Quite clearly, the pure scale would be impossible on a fixed-pitch instrument with twelve different notes in an octave, since what is true of the scale beginning on C is true for every other scale, and discrepancies will not only exist within scales but between them too.

Discussion could continue, but sufficient information has been produced to show that tempering is inevitable. One final example will show some of the problems of pitching the note F sharp, in the scale of C. To fulfil the conditions stated below, it would need to have the following cent values if it were to be true on each occasion:

1	As a major third above D	590 cents
2	As a chromatic semitone below G	632 cents
3	As a true argmented fourth above C	568 cents

On a modern keyboard, F sharp would have a cent value of 600, in relation to C, whatever its function. This list covers only some of the conditions affecting one note; at some time or another all notes could be similarly affected depending on the circumstances under which they are used.

3
HOW TO TEMPER

Having established that there are problems and then having isolated them, the next logical step is to attempt some means of solution. It is here, however, that the particular and the general come into conflict. Just as all knowledge is particular, no matter how general its application so all tempering is particular and not general. Tempering can only be done to a particular instrument, at a particular time and by a particular person, which makes generalisation about it difficult. On the other hand, launching too quickly into details about particular instruments must lead to repetition when those instruments are dealt with in more depth. Since there are two main aspects of tempering, namely the static and the flexible, some form of compromise can be effected by demonstrating some of the general principles of tempering in relation to keyboard and stringed instruments.

The static form of tempering is that which applies to any instrument on which the notes are fixed, and limited to a certain number (usually twelve, but not invariably so) of different, but not easily alterable, steps within an octave. The main instruments in this category are keyboards, fretted instruments (guitars, viols, etc) and the harp, although instruments with finger holes, keys or valves, are, to some extent, similarly affected.

The problem is most acute on keyboards and the harp, where, physically, the hands of the performer are occupied in selecting notes, the pitches of which have all been pre-ordained by a tuner, whether that tuner be the performer or not. The difficulties inherent in trying to supply a keyboard instrument with a scale which will render it playable even in one key have already been explored, but it has always been the tuner's task to make instruments acceptable in all keys, or at least as many as possible, by whatever the method currently in favour.

Fashions have changed over the centuries as to what is, or is not, acceptable in keyboard tuning. On a modern piano, it would not be considered reasonable to have some chords better in tune

HOW TO TEMPER 35

than others. Equality in tuning is the present fashion, but this may not, or indeed should not, meet with the approval of performers on early keyboard instruments. Many of these instruments reached their maturity long before equal temperament was in common use.

Whatever the type of tempering in fashion, the most usual method of tuning keyboard instruments is to tune in pure octaves and tempered fourths and fifths. To decide on how much the fourths and fifths are to be tempered, the quality of the major thirds needs to be considered. The nearer the thirds are to true, the flatter the fifths and sharper the fourths must be. To find out why this must be so, cent values are helpful. By tuning upwards in pure fifths from a note C, after four such fifths have been tuned, namely C - G, G - D, D - A and A - E, the final note is an E, two octaves and a major third above the starting note, which, shown in figures, is

$$702 \text{ cents} \times 4 = 2808 \text{ cents}$$

By deducting two octaves, the major third produced will be 2808 cents minus 2400 cents, or 408 cents.

Although this is strictly speaking correct, a tuner does not work in this way. Since the interval of a fourth is the inversion of a fifth, by using both fourths and fifths, it is much easier to keep the notes to be tuned within an octave, or just a little more, which keeps the beat rates of the notes being tuned closer together, allowing for more accurate listening and comparison. A more likely sequence of tuning would therefore be, tune up a fifth from C to G, then down an octave from G to low G, then up a fifth from low G to D, down a fourth from D to A, and finally up a fifth from A to E. The final note is then a major third above the note on which the tuning sequence began. Shown in figures, that tuning sequence is:

```
C - G    702 cents
G - G    702 minus 1200 cents = -498 cents
G - D   -498 plus   702 cents =  204 cents
D - A    204 minus  498 cents = -294 cents
A - E   -294 plus   702 cents =  408 cents
```

The result is the same, a major third of 408 cents is produced. This is called a Pythagorean third and it is a syntonic comma, or 22 cents, greater than a true major third of 386 cents. To arrive at a true major third by tuning in pure octaves and tempered fifths and fourths, each fifth must be tempered by a quarter of a syntonic comma, on the narrow side, making each fourth a quarter of a syntonic comma too wide. Since a quarter of 22 cents is 5.5 cents, each fifth then needs to be 696.5 cents and each fourth 503.5 cents. Tuning in these intervals and pure octaves gives the following figures:

   C - G   696.5 cents
   G - G   696.5 minus 1200   cents = −503.5 cents
   G - D   −503.5 plus   696.5 cents = 193   cents
   D - A   193   minus   503.5 cents = −310.5 cents
   A - E   −310.5 plus   696.5 cents = 386   cents

These two sets of figures show the truth of the generalisation that pure fifths produce wide thirds, and pure thirds require narrow fifths, in keyboard tempering. The first method, if continued, produces the Pythagorean scale, while the second set produces the meantone scale, the particular type of meantone being known as ¼-comma meantone.

Equal temperament, the method of keyboard tempering which became standard in England in the middle of the nineteenth century and is still in use today, stems from a different root. The Pythagorean scale, based on tuning in pure fifths, fourths and octaves, produces wide major thirds. The meantone system divides the syntonic comma equally among a certain number of fifths, producing major thirds which are either pure (¼-comma meantone) or slightly wide (⅕-comma meantone), but at the expense of certain intervals and chords which are well out of tune (the 'wolves'). Equal temperament is based on dividing the comma of Pythagoras. If, starting from any note on a keyboard, a series of perfect fifths is built, after twelve fifths the original starting note, or one of its octaves, will again be reached and each of the twelve notes of the chromatic scale will have been touched once. The series, beginning on C, would run as follows:

   C - G - A - E - B - F♯ - C♯ - G♯ - D♯ - A♯ - E♯(F) - B♯ (C)

It is noticeable, however, that enharmonic changes need to be made if the written series is to end on C. But making these changes tends to obscure the fact that B sharp, when tuned in this fashion, will be 24 cents higher than the note C which represents it on a keyboard. To get rid of this 24 cent error among twelve fifths can be simply achieved by taking two cents from each fifth. This obvious expedient will make the system cyclic; twelve fifths will fit exactly into seven octaves.

Translating the initial steps of the system into cent values, the following figures now emerge. A pure fifth of 702 cents reduced by 2 cents, produces a tempered fifth of 700 cents:

C - G   700 cents
G - G   700 minus 1200 cents = −500 cents
G - D   −500 plus   700 cents =   200 cents
D - A   200 minus   500 cents = −300 cents
A - E   −300 plus   700 cents =   400 cents

By keeping the fourths (500 cents instead of 498), and the fifths (700 cents instead of 702) very close to true, and holding the octaves exactly true, equal temperament produces wide major thirds (400 cents instead of 386), and narrow minor thirds (300 cents instead of 316), but has the advantage of fitting the slightly flat fifths and the pure octaves exactly together, making every major and minor key equally in (or out of) tune and getting rid of the very sharp thirds of the Pythagorean scale and the 'wolves' of meantone.

Only the initial steps of the various tunings have so far been described. To construct a keyboard scale, twelve such steps must be taken. The Pythagorean scale is not suitable as a keyboard scale which acts both harmonically and melodically. Its wide major thirds are poor when used in an harmonic context, and if the initial steps were continued to twelve, they will produce the discrepancy of a Pythagorean comma between the octaves and the fifths. Melodically, however, the scale is useful, and is, in part, used by singers and stringed instrument players today. It is used in part, because having the facility to depart from it to a tempered scale when its deficiencies would begin to show allows a flexibility denied the rigid scale of a keyboard.

The meantone system is based on division of the syntonic comma. Only ¼-comma meantone has so far been mentioned, but it is possible to divide the syntonic comma in many ways. It can at least be divided into ten parts, but to divide it into eleven equal parts would make each of those parts 2 cents, and subtracting 2 cents from a pure fifth of 702 cents, leaves an equally tempered fifth of 700 cents. Equal temperament and $\frac{1}{11}$-comma meantone are therefore the same thing. There are other useful divisions of the syntonic comma which have had supporters in various centuries. Two of the most used are, perhaps, ⅕-comma and ⅙-comma temperings.

The initial steps of ⅕-comma would be as follows. Dividing the syntonic comma by five gives 4.4 cents, which means that in ⅕-comma meantone the fifths are made narrower by 4.4 cents (which makes them 697.6 cents), and the fourths are widened by the same amount (making them 502.4 cents):

C - G   697.6 cents
G - G   697.6 minus 1200   = −502.4 cents
G - D   −502.4 plus   697.6 =   195.2 cents
D - A   195.2 minus   502.4 = −307.2 cents
A - E   −307.2 plus   697.6 =   390.4 cents

The major third of 390.4 cents is ⅕ of a syntonic comma wider than true, but the temperament has the advantage of fourths and fifths which are slightly better than ¼-comma meantone, as well as slightly less ferocious 'wolves'.

The initial steps of ⅙-comma meantone can be calculated by deducting ⅙ of a syntonic comma (3.67 cents) from a pure fifth (698.33 cents) and adding it to a pure fourth (501.67 cents):

C - G   698.33 cents
G - G   698.33 minus 1200   = −501.67 cents
G - D   −501.67 plus   698.33 =   196.66 cents
D - A   196.66 minus   501.67 = −305.01 cents
A - E   −305.01 plus   698.33 =   393.32 cents

The major third of ⅙-comma meantone, at 7.32 cents wider than true, is just a little more than half way between a true and an equally tempered major third.

It is simple enough to work out calculations on paper, but in the act of tuning figures have to be translated into sound. Tuners usually tune in fifths, fourths and octaves and check the accuracy of their tuning in thirds and sixths. The system used must be extremely accurate, because the difference between a pure fifth (which, if used in tuning, produces the unpleasantly wide Pythagorean third) and the ¼-comma meantone fifth (which produces pure major thirds) is only 5½ cents, and the difference between pure and equally tempered fifths is only two cents. There is no room for approximation, or the resultant tuning will be some sort of hybrid, having the characteristics of many different systems.

The professional tuner's method is to count beats, or, more

correctly, to recognise beat rates. During apprenticeship or training, a tuner would be taught to listen for beats, and be instructed on the beat rates to accept for fifths, fourths, thirds and sixths. This training is based on equal temperament; few tuners are required to use any other form of tempering. Performers on keyboard instruments other than pianos normally tune their own instruments. Because of their construction, harpsichords, clavichords, virginals and spinets (the true spinet, not the square piano) tend to go out of tune quite quickly, and calling in a tuner on every occasion when they need to be tuned is both inconvenient and expensive. It is on these instruments and the organ that temperaments other than equal are most appropriate. For this reason, organ tuners are now taking an interest in tuning to a variety of temperaments, and the services of such specialists is available in some areas.

To assist those who wish to tune in other temperaments than the usual equal temperament, it is possible simply to give beat rates for the scales of some of the most common temperings, and for those who do not wish to calculate beat rates for themselves, this has been done in the Appendix. However, a much wider range of temperaments can be attempted by anyone who is able and willing to do the simple calculations necessary. A calculator is probably the most useful aid in this respect, but log tables are sufficient.

The information which follows is on how to temper. Although it does not relate to a particular instrument directly, it is most appropriate for keyboard instruments. Calculation stems from translating the scale to be set into cent values, or from a description of that temperament given accurately enough to enable it to be translated into cent values. Perfect fifths and fourths as well as major thirds and sixths are required at some stage in the setting of a temperament. Accordingly, information on how to calculate beat rates is given for all of these intervals.

Tempering perfect fifths

The principle of listening for and recognising beats has already been discussed; tuning depends on the ability to put these skills into action. A perfect fifth is tuned pure by making the third harmonic of the lower note coincide exactly with the second harmonic of the upper. In tempering, the amount of mistuning required is judged at the same pitch as the unanimity of harmonics of the pure interval. The general must now again give way to the particular, because it is not possible to give precise instructions on tuning a fifth in general; this is only possible for a particular fifth. The most usual place to begin is the $c' - g'$ fifth. From a standard tuning fork, the frequency of c' is 261.62 Hertz. For a pure fifth the ratio between the two notes is as 2:3, or as 1:1.5, therefore the frequency for a pure g' above c' at 261.62 Hertz is 261.62 Hertz multiplied by 1.5, or 392.43 Hertz.

In an equally tempered scale, every semitone is equal; therefore an equally tempered fifth will be 700 cents. A pure fifth of 702 cents has the ratio as 1:1.5; by converting 700 cents into a ratio it would be possible to find the frequency for an equally tempered g'.

In the words of A. J. Ellis, who devised the cent value system for describing intervals, 'cents are in fact a system of logs in which log 2 equals 1200'. In one octave there are twelve semitones, each of which may be considered to be divided into 100 equal parts. The cent values are defined such that they are in direct porportion to the common logarithms of the corresponding vibration ratio. This ratio for notes one octave apart is 2:1. Therefore we define

$$\text{value } \log_{10} 2 = 1200 \text{ cents}$$
$$\text{value } 1 = 1200 \div \log_{10} 2$$
$$= 3986.3136 \text{ cents}$$

This may be used as a multiplying factor to convert ratios into cent values. Hence ratio 3:2 may be converted as follows:

$$\log_{10} 1.5 = 3986.3136 \times \log_{10} 1.5 \text{ cents}$$
$$= 3986.3136 \times 0.17609 \text{ cents}$$
$$= 701.953 \text{ cents.}$$

Similarly, to convert cents into ratios,

$$\log_{10} (\text{ratio}) = \text{no. cents} \div 3986.3136$$
$$\log_{10} r = 701.953 \div 3986.3136$$
$$= 0.17609$$
$$r = \text{antilog } 0.17609$$
$$= 1.5$$
$$\text{ratio is } 1.5:1$$
$$\text{or } 3:2$$

Taking the equally tempered fifth of 700 cents, the ratio between the two notes which form it can be calculated as follows:

700 cents divided by 3986.3136 = .17560
Antilog of .17560 = 1.49831

The ratio between the two notes forming an equally tempered fifth will be as 1:1.49831. To calculate the frequency for an equally tempered g', 261.62 Hertz must be multiplied by 1.49831, making 391.99 Hertz. There are now two frequencies for g'. The difference between these frequencies at g' is 392.43 minus 391.99 Hertz, or .44 Hertz. The interval between these two pitches for g' is very small, less than half a vibration per second. If the two notes c' and g' are struck together, and the upper note is tuned to 391.99 Hertz, no discrepancy will be heard at that pitch, as Example 6 shows.

Example 6 Showing the position and size of discrepancy in an equally tempered fifth $c'-g'$. Harmonics are shown as guides

The lower note of the fifth, having a frequency of 261.62 Hertz, will produce as its second and third harmonics the notes c'' and g'' marked in the example as guides, with the frequencies stated. There is no harmonic formed by c' at pitch g'. The upper note of the fifth has been tuned to a frequency of 391.99 Hertz, and its second harmonic, with frequency, is shown. The pitch at which the harmonics of these notes first coincide is g'', and it is here that a discrepancy will show. (Discrepancies will obviously appear at higher frequencies too, but these will be less loud, and though heard and recognised by the tuner, will be disregarded during tuning.) The discrepancy between the two pitches for g' will be heard at pitch g'' as a beat of .8848 per second, a little more than 1½ beats in two seconds. This is not an easy beat rate to recognise, but it can be sensed immediately by using a metronome. A metronome setting of 60 gives one pulse per second; a metronome setting of 60 multiplied by .88 will therefore give a pulse rate of .88 beats per second. Such a setting works out at 52.8; a metronome setting of 53 being near enough for all practical purposes.

From this information, the steps involved in tuning an equally tempered fifth can be formulated. The first is to set c' at 261.62 Hertz from a tuning fork. This being done, the second is to tune

g' as a pure fifth above it, making sure that there are no audible beats at pitch g''. The third step is to set a metronome at 53, feel the pulsations at this speed, then lower the note g' until the beating heard at pitch g'' coincides in speed with the metronome. The fifth has then been accurately tuned as an equally tempered perfect fifth.

The calculation of beat rates for fifths in other temperaments is done in a similar fashion to those in equal temperament. The stages of calculation will be shown this time with reference to ¼-comma meantone.

Stage 1 From a description of the temperament, calculate the size of a fifth in cents. In ¼-comma meantone, each fifth is made flat by one quarter of a syntonic comma. A syntonic comma is 22 cents, a quarter of it must therefore be 5.5 cents; by deducting this from the cent value for a pure fifth, the size of a ¼-comma meantone fifth will be 696.5 cents.

Stage 2 From the cent value of the fifth, the ratio between the two notes which form it now have to be calculated. This is done by using the multiplying factor previously established.

696.5 cents divided by 3986.3136 = .17472
Antilog of   .17472 = 1.49528

The ratio between the two notes forming the fifth is as 1:1.49528.

Stage 3 This stage changes the general into the particular. Taking, for the sake of convenience and comparison, the same fifth as before, $c' - g'$, the frequency of c', 261.62 Hertz, is multiplied in accordance with the ratio as 1:1.49528. This makes the frequency of a ¼-comma meantone g' 391.2 Hertz (261.62 Hertz × 1.49528).

Stage 4 In this stage, the frequency of the ¼-comma meantone fifth is subtracted from that of a pure fifth above c', to find the discrepancy between the two values for g'. 392.43 Hertz minus 391.2 Hertz gives a discrepancy of 1.23 Hertz at pitch g'.

Stage 5 This is the final stage in which the discrepancy at pitch g' is converted into a beat rate heard at pitch g''. Since g' is an octave lower than g'', the size of the discrepancy at pitch g' will be doubled when heard at g''. The beat rate will therefore be 2.46 beats per second, which, converted into a metronome setting, is 2.46 multiplied by 60, or 147.6, a metronome setting of 148 being acceptable for all practical purposes.

Having gone through the stages of calculating the beat rate for

HOW TO TEMPER 43

a ¼-comma meantone fifth, to tune one accurately is a similar process to that described for the equally tempered fifth, the only difference being that the metronome setting in this case is 148. The frequencies of the two notes which form a perfect fifth must vary as the pitches of the notes vary. A metronome setting of 53 gives the beat rate for an equally tempered fifth $c' - g'$, but it will not do for any other equally tempered fifth. The ratio of 1:1.49831, however, will apply to every equally tempered fifth. It is therefore unnecessary to go through all the stages of calculation once the ratio of the two notes forming a fifth in the temperament has been established. To tune the fifth $g' - d'$ in equal temperament, for instance, only requires stages 3 - 5 of the process outlined once the frequency of g has been established. Since the temperament being described at the moment is equal temperament, note g must be calculated as a pure octave below an equally tempered g', which means that the frequency for g', 391.99 Hertz, must be halved. This makes the frequency for note g, 195.99 Hertz. Carrying on now as from stage 3, the following calculations are made.

Stage 3 An equally tempered d' above this newly established g would be 195.99 Hertz multiplied by 1.49831, which equals 293.65 Hertz, but a pure d' above it would have the frequency 195.99 Hertz multiplied by 1.5, which is 293.98 Hertz.

Stage 4 The frequency of the equally tempered fifth is subtracted from that of the pure fifth to establish the size of the discrepancy at d'. The difference between 293.65 Hertz and 293.98 Hertz is .33 Hertz.

Stage 5 This is the final stage in which the discrepancy at pitch d' is converted into a beat rate. The beating caused by this discrepancy would be heard an octave higher, at d'', which would give a beat rate of .66 beats per second. Converting this into a metronome setting by multiplying it by 60 gives a setting of 39.6. This is a very slow rate and the lower the beat the less accurate the swing of the metronome. At such a speed it is safer to set the metronome at twice the speed, actually 79.2, but 80 would be near enough, and count each alternate swing of the metronome as the beat rate.

Having established the ratio for a perfect fifth, every other fifth in the tuning series can be calculated, the frequency of each note may be established and beat rates to assist tuning set by a metronome.

Tempering perfect fourths

As already explained, a tuner uses perfect fourths as well as fifths. Tempering a perfect fourth is similar to the process for tempering a fifth, but not precisely so. Since the harmonics which the two notes forming a perfect fourth have in common are at a higher pitch, the beat rate will be faster than for a fifth. Calculation is again in five stages, as follows:

Stage 1 From a description of the temperament, calculate the value of a fourth in cents. In equal temperament each fourth is 500 cents, because every semitone in the temperament is 100 cents and a fourth, c' to f', contains five semitones.

Stage 2 From the cent value of the fourth, the ratio between the two notes which form it can be calculated. This is done by using the multiplying factor.

500 cents divided by 3986.3136 = .12542
Antilog of   .12542 = 1.33484

Therefore the ratio between the two notes forming an equally tempered perfect fourth is as 1:1.33484, whereas the ratio between two notes forming a pure perfect fourth is as 3:4, or 1:1.3333.

Stage 3 This stage brings the calculation to a particular fourth. For the sake of convenience and comparison, the fourth $c' - f'$ will be used. Two frequencies for f' can be calculated from the two different ratios. A pure fourth from c' would have the frequency 261.62 Hertz multiplied by 1.3333, which is 348.81, an equally tempered fourth from the same note would have the frequency 261.62 Hertz multiplied by 1.33484, or 349.22 Hertz.

Stage 4 In this stage the difference between the two frequencies for f' is found. 349.22 Hertz minus 348.81 Hertz gives a discrepancy of .41 Hertz at pitch f'.

Stage 5 The final stage involves calculating the beat rate at the pitch where harmonics in common between the notes forming the fourth should coincide. In the case of the fourth $c' - f'$, that pitch is c''' (the fourth harmonic of c' and the third of f'). to calculate the beat rate at this pitch, it is necessary only to multiply the descrepancy at pitch f' by three, since the beating will be heard at the pitch of the third harmonic from that note. Multiplying .41 by three gives a beat rate of 1.23 at pitch c''', which, when multiplied by 60 gives a metronome setting of 73.8, a considerable increase over the beat rate for the fifth $c' - g'$.

When tuning a fourth, it must be remembered that the

tempering is on the wide rather than the narrow side. Tuning the tempered fourth $c' - f'$ therefore entails tuning it, in the first instance, as a pure fourth with no audible beating at pitch c'''. When this has been done, a beat rate is taken from the metronome set at 74, and the pitch of f' is raised until the beating at pitch c''' coincides with the pulsations of the metronome.

Tempering major thirds
Major thirds are used either in the tuning system itself or as checks on the accuracy of the tuning by using other intervals. It matters little in which of these ways the third is used, but the method of calculating its beat rate is still important.

The tempering of a major third is done in a similar fashion to that already described, the difference lying only in the pitch of the harmonic which the two notes concerned first have in common. The process is in five stages.

Stage 1 This stage involves finding the size of the interval, in cents, from a description of the temperament. In equal temperament a major third will be 400 cents.

Stage 2 From the cent value, the ratio between the two notes forming the interval can be calculated by using the multiplying factor:

400 cents divided by 3986.3136 = .10034
Antilog of .10034 = 1.25992

The ratio between the two notes forming an equally tempered major third is therefore as 1:1.25992.

Stage 3 As before, this stage moves from the general to the particular. Again taking c' as a starting point, a major third would be $c' - e'$, therefore two frequencies for e' need to be found, firstly a pure major third above c' and secondly an equally tempered major third above c'. Since the ratio for the two notes forming a major third is as 4:5, or as 1:1.25, a pure e' above c' has the frequency 261.62 multiplied by 1.25, which is 327.025 Hertz. An equally tempered major third above c' has the frequency 261.62 Hertz multiplied by 1.25992, or 329.62 Hertz.

Stage 4 At this stage the discrepancy at pitch e' is calculated by subtracting the two values for this note. Subtracting 327.025 Hertz from 329.62 Hertz gives a discrepancy of 2.595 Hertz at pitch e'.

Stage 5 In this final stage, the discrepancy at pitch e' is converted into a beat rate heard at pitch e''', the first harmonic which c' and e' have in common. Since this is two octaves above e' the beat rate will be 2.595 multiplied by 4, or 10.38 beats per second, which, when multiplied by 60 to give a metronome setting, makes such a setting 622.8! An impression of this very fast beat rate can be gained from a metronome by setting it at just less than 208, the fastest setting on a standard metronome, and imagining three subdivisions of each pulsation of the metronome.

This fast beat rate is the reason for the 'shimmer' on equally tempered thirds and sixths, a shimmer which some musicians think adds 'life' to keyboard chords, but which others believe gives them an unacceptable coarseness, especially on organs and harpsichords. An equally tempered third is by no means as coarse as a Pythagorean major third, produced by tuning in pure fifths. Its beat rate can be calculated by going through the five steps used for other intervals. Now that the steps are known, the calculation can be done in continuous fashion, saving time and space in description. A Pythagorean major third is 408 cents:

408 cents divided by 3986.3136 = .10235
Antilog of   .10235 = 1.26576

The ratio of the two notes forming a Pythagorean major third is as 1:1.26576. Taking this ratio for the $c' - e'$ major third:

261.62 multiplied by 1.26576 = 331.15

This gives e' a frequency of 331.15 Hertz. A pure major third above c' has been calculated as 327.025 Hertz, making the difference between these two values at e' 4.125 Hertz. This would be heard as a discrepancy at pitch e''', two octaves higher, giving a beat rate at that pitch of 16.5 beats per second. When this is multiplied by 60 it gives a metronome setting of 990!

Trying to imagine a beat rate of this speed makes it clear why Pythagorean major thirds are not acceptable harmonically. As for the equally tempered major third, most tuners learn to feel a beat rate of just under eleven beats per second, and then, starting from c', tune a third with this beat rate above it. Having done this, they tune in fifths and fourths to arrive at the e' already set. Thus, accuracy of the first few intervals can be established.

Tempering major sixths
Unlike the major third, the major sixth is seldom, if ever, actually used in setting the initial octave of the scale, but since it

HOW TO TEMPER

is such a useful check, it is desirable that the means of calculating it should be given. Again, it seems best to give a continuous description rather than breaking it down into steps. The only two pieces of information required at first are the cent value for an equally tempered major sixth and the ratio for a true one. The cent value is 900 cents, and the ratio is 3:5 or 1:1.66666. Calculating from c' at 261.62 Hertz, the frequency for a pure major sixth above it is 261.62 multiplied by 1.666666, or 436.03331 Hertz. To convert 900 cents into a ratio:

900 cents divided by 3986.3136 = .22577
Antilog of .22577 = 1.68179

The ratio for an equally tempered major sixth is therefore 1:1.68179. Multiplying this by 261.62 Hertz, gives a frequency of 439.99 Hertz. This gives the two values for a', a major sixth above c', as 436.03 and 439.99 Hertz respectively. Subtracting these two frequencies gives a discrepancy of 3.96 Hertz at pitch a'. This will be heard as a beat rate at pitch e''', making that beat rate 3.96 multiplied by 3, or 11.88 beats per second at pitch e'''. This is equivalent to a metronome setting of 712.8. An equally tempered major sixth will consequently beat faster than a major third tuned from the same note, although the beating will be heard at the same pitch.

In ¼-comma meantone a major sixth, unlike a major third, is not pure but a quarter of a syntonic comma too wide. Its cent value is therefore 889.5 cents. Calculating continuously, the ratio between the two notes forming it will be

889.5 divided by 3986.3136 = .22313
Antilog of .22313 = 1.67162,

which makes the ratio 1:1.67162. The frequency of a ¼-comma meantone a' above c' at 261.62 Hertz will be 261.62 Hertz multiplied by 1.67162, or 437.33 Hertz. A true a' above c' has already been calculated as 436.03 Hertz, making the discrepancy at a' 1.3 Hertz. This will be heard as a beat rate of 3.9 at pitch e''', equivalent to a metronome setting of 234. Although this is a fast beat rate, an equally tempered major sixth beats more than three times as fast.

The calculations for tempering have been repeated a few times to enable anyone wishing to work out beat rates for tuning any temperament to become familiar with the process. The steps have so far been given in relation to specific calculations; below, they are given in the abstract.

Step 1 From a description of the temperament to be set, work out the cent value of appropriate intervals for setting the scale.

Step 2 From the cent value of the interval required, work out the ratio between the notes which form it as well as the ratio between the notes of the same interval were it to be tuned true.

Step 3 This step moves from the general to the particular. From the frequency of the lower note of the interval, calculate the two values of the upper note, and also whether the tempered value is less than, or greater than, the true value.

Step 4 Find the difference between these two frequencies at the pitch of the upper note.

Step 5 Find the lowest pitch at which the two notes forming the interval have a harmonic in common. Multiply the figure found in step four by the appropriate number to find the beat rate at the pitch of the common harmonic, the multiplying factor being 2 for an octave, 3 for a twelfth, 4 for a double octave, etc, and finally, to establish a metronome setting, multiply the beat rate at the common harmonic by 60.

Knowing how to work out beat rates is fine, but to a tuner, the complete scheme for laying a scale is of much greater interest and utility. The method of calculation is useful, but the essential matter, from the point of view of laying a scale, is to know the beat rates for crucial intervals and checks. Space forbids any attempt to give fully worked out details for many temperaments, but it is possible to do this for one temperament, and from it, work out a summary of the essential details. The temperament chosen here is ¼-comma meantone; in the chapter specifically concerned with keyboard tuning, information about many other temperaments will be given in summarised form.

Full information for setting a ¼-comma meantone scale
Before any frequencies are established it saves time if the ratios between the intervals which are to be used in setting the scale are calculated and set down. Two sets of ratios are needed, those for pure intervals and those for the same intervals when tempered. Since the calculations are correct to eight figures, the cent values for various intervals, which have previously been given to the nearest whole or half cent, are no longer appropriate if the figures, when moving towards pure intervals, are to give an accurate picture. The cent values for pure intervals must first be

calculated, and then the correct ¼-comma meantone values derived from them.

The correct cent value for a pure fifth is:

$$\log 1.5 = .17609$$
$$.17609 \times 3986.3136 = 701.95394 \text{ cents}$$

The correct cent value for a pure fourth is:

$$\log 1.3333333 = .12493$$
$$.12493 \times 3986.3136 = 498.04603 \text{ cents}$$

The correct cent value for a pure major third is:

$$\log 1.25 = .09691$$
$$.09691 \times 3986.3136 = 386.31365 \text{ cents}$$

The correct cent value for a pure major sixth is:

$$\log 1.6666666 = .22184$$
$$.22184 \times 3986.3136 = 884.35968 \text{ cents}$$

The correct cent value for a syntonic comma is:

$$\log 1.0125 = .0053950$$
$$.0053950 \times 3986.3136 = 21.506281 \text{ cents}$$

A quarter of a syntonic comma will therefore be:

$$21.506281 \text{ cents} \div 4 = 5.3765702 \text{ cents}$$

The ratios for intervals involved in setting the scale will therefore be:

Interval	Pure	¼-comma
Major third	1:1.25	1:1.25
Perfect fifth	1:1.5	1:1.49535
Perfect fourth	1:1.3333333	1:1.33748
Major sixth	1:1.6666666	1:1.67185
Octave	1:2	1:2

Using the above information, and starting from a tuning fork giving pitch c'' at 523.24 Hertz, calculation for the setting of a scale can proceed. The following symbols have been used on the musical stave. The note to be tuned is shown as a crotchet without a tail (.), and this also denotes the pitch of the discrepancy shown in column 5. The note to listen for when tuning is shown as a guide (w), and this also shows the pitch at

Table 1 Complete calculations for setting ¼-comma meantone

Step	Interval	Pure	¼-comma	Discrepancy	Beat rate	Metronome
1	c''	523.24	523.24	0	0	–
2	$c'' - c'$	523.24 ÷ 2 = 261.62	523.24 ÷ 2 = 261.62	0	0	–
3	$c' - g'$	261.62 × 1.5 = 392.43	261.62 × 1.49535 = 391.21346	1.21654	2.43308	146
4	$g' - g$		391.21346 ÷ 2 = 195.60673	0	0	–
5	$g - d'$	195.60673 × 1.5 = 293.41009	195.60673 × 1.49535 = 292.50052	.90957	1.81914	109
6	$d' - a$	292.50052 ÷ 1.3̇3̇ = 219.37544	292.50052 ÷ 1.33748 = 218.69524	.6802	2.7208	163
7	$a - e'$	218.69524 × 1.5 = 328.04286	218.69524 × 1.49535 = 327.02592	1.01694	2.03388	122
8	$c' - e'$	261.62 × 1.25 = 327.025	327.02592	0	0	–
9	$e' - b$	327.02592 ÷ 1.3̇3̇ = 245.26944	327.02592 ÷ 1.33748 = 244.50901	.76043	3.04172	183
10	$g - b$	195.60673 × 1.25 = 244.50841	244.50901	0	0	–
11	$b - f\sharp'$	244.50901 × 1.5 = 366.76351	244.50901 × 1.49535 = 365.62654	1.13697	2.27394	136
12	$d' - f\sharp'$	292.50052 × 1.25 = 365.62565	365.62654	0	0	–
13	$f\sharp' - c\sharp'$	365.62654 ÷ 1.333 = 274.21991	365.62654 ÷ 1.33748 = 273.36972	.85019	3.40076	204
14	$a - c\sharp'$	218.69524 × 1.25 = 273.36905	273.36972	0	0	–
15	$c\sharp' - g\sharp'$	273.36972 ÷ 1.333 = 205.02729	273.36972 ÷ 1.33748 = 204.39163	.63566	2.54264	153
16	$c' - f$	261.62 ÷ 1.5 = 174.41333	261.62 ÷ 1.49535 = 174.95569	.54236	1.62708	98
17	$f - a$	174.95569 × 1.25 = 218.69461	218.69524	0	0	–
18	$f - b\flat$	174.95569 × 1.3̇3̇ = 233.27424	174.95569 × 1.33748 = 233.99973	.72549	2.17647	131
19	$b\flat - d'$	233.99973 × 1.25 = 292.49966	292.50052	0	0	–
20	$b\flat - e\flat'$	233.99973 × 1.3̇3̇ = 311.99963	233.99973 × 1.33748 = 312.96995	.97032	2.91096	175
21	$e\flat' - g'$	312.96995 × 1.25 = 391.21243	391.21346	0	0	–
22	$g\flat - e\sharp'$	204.39163 × 1.5 = 306.58744	312.96995	6.38251	12.76502	766

N.B. Bold figures indicate checks

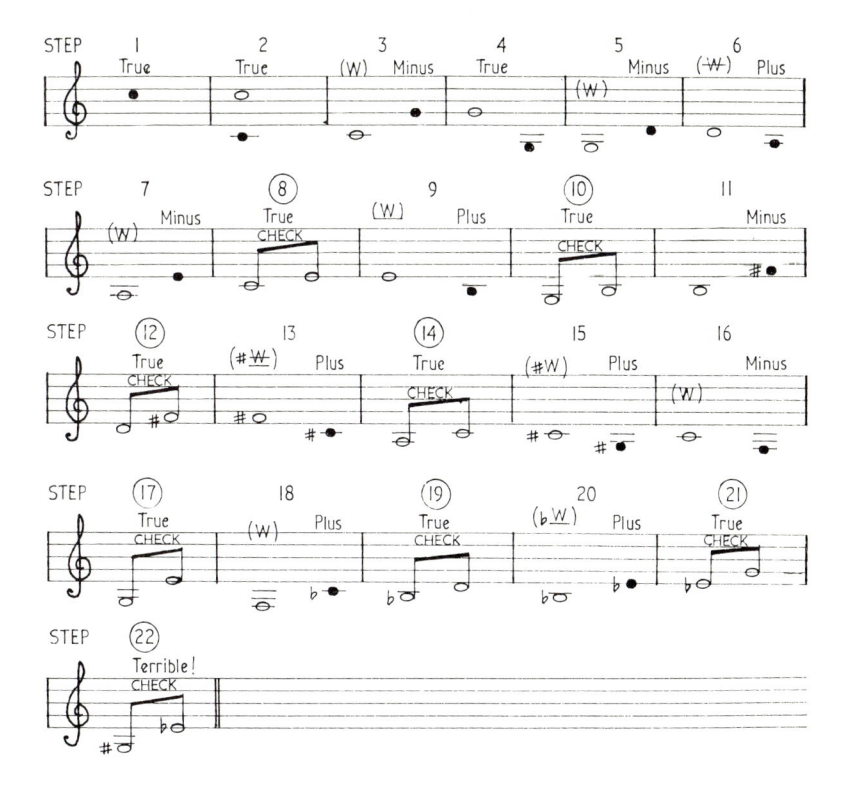

which to listen for beat rates given in column 6. The pairs of minims joined by a tail (♫) denote an interval to use as a check for accuracy. The terms true, plus and minus, refer to the size of the interval. True means what it says. Plus means that the interval is to be made wider than true, minus means that it is to be made narrower than true. Remember that widening an interval does not always mean sharpening the note being tuned. It depends on whether that note is above or below the note from which the tuning is taking place. If the note to be tuned is above, then widening means sharpening it, but if it is below, widening the interval means flattening the note. Similar precautions are necessary when making an interval narrow.

The setting of this scale has been given with only seven checks for accuracy. An experienced tuner may well wish to use more. For someone who is a beginner, or who has little experience, too many instructions tend to confuse. Seven checks, although not lavish, are adequate, but the topic requires further discussion. See the above table.

Summary of setting ¼-comma meantone

Step		Interval	Size	Beats/sec	Metronome
1	tune	c''	true	0	–
2	tune	$c'' - c'$	true	0	–
3	tune	$c' - g'$	narrow	2.43	146
4	tune	$g' - g$	true	0	–
5	tune	$g - d'$	narrow	1.82	109
6	tune	$d' - a$	wide	2.72	163
7	tune	$a - e'$	narrow	2.03	122
8	check	$c' - e'$	true	0	–
9	tune	$e' - b$	wide	3.04	183
10	check	$g - b$	true	0	–
11	tune	$b - f\sharp'$	narrow	2.27	136
12	check	$d' - f\sharp'$	true	0	–
13	tune	$f\sharp' - c\sharp'$	wide	3.4	204
14	check	$a - c\sharp'$	true	0	–
15	tune	$c\sharp' - g\sharp'$	wide	2.54	153
16	tune	$c' - f$	narrow	1.63	98
17	check	$f - a$	true	0	–
18	tune	$f - b\flat$	wide	2.18	131
19	check	$b\flat - d'$	true	0	–
20	tune	$b\flat - e\flat'$	wide	2.91	175
21	check	$e\flat' - g'$	true	0	–
22	check	$g\flat - e\sharp'$	wide	12.77	766

It is essential when using this summary to adjust the tuning note (ie the right hand note in the 'interval' column) in the proper direction to make the interval wider or narrower than true. To make sure, each note should be tuned true at first, then moved in the appropriate direction. To minimise the possibility of error, all the tempered notes as far as step 15 need to be lowered to move them in the right direction, and all those from step 16 to step 20 need to be raised.

Alternative methods

The professional tuners work by listening for beat rates, but there are other ways of tuning a keyboard instrument. One of the most likely is trial and error. With a temperament like ¼-comma meantone, such a method is not too difficult, because all that is required is to fit four perfect fifths into a series which will form a pure major third. It can be done, starting at c', in the following fashion. Tune $c' - e'$, true. Starting again at c', tune $c' - g'$ true, and then flatten g' a little. Tune down an octave to g true. Tune up a true fifth to d', flatten it a little. Tune up another fifth, $d' - a'$, true, and then flatten it a little. Tune down a true octave,

$a' - a$. Test the fifth $a - e'$. If it is about as narrow as the $g - d'$ fifth, and the $c' - g'$ and $d' - a'$ fifths are similarly narrow while the major third $c' - e'$ remains true, then all that is left to do is to tune in true major thirds from the notes set, checking the fifths produced to make sure they are similarly narrow. If the first group of fifths which formed the major third was not correct when tested by the trial of the $a - e'$ fifth, then they all need to be adjusted until they are equally narrow. Since there are only four of them, this is not too difficult a task. Other temperaments can be set in a similar fashion, but the method is not very safe, and can be very frustrating.

A more modern method is to buy a tone meter. This is an instrument which can be adjusted to give notes of almost any pitch within an octave, or slightly more than an octave, depending on the type and cost of the instrument. The more sophisticated of them will even check beat rates for the operator, showing how far wrong a note is and whether it is too sharp or too flat, while the less costly will give a note of the correct cent value in relation to a given starting note, leaving the operator the task of tuning the keyboard note to be in exact unison with it. Such devices would seem to be the answer to tuning difficulties, but, as always, there are snags. Firstly, unisons are not so easy to tune as they appear to be; it is much easier to be sure of a regular moving beat than it is to be sure that there is no beat present at all. Secondly, a tone meter can only give an accurate mathematical reading, and such a reading is only correct if all the factors involved are correct. For instance, it cannot allow for any discrepancies there might be in the instrument being tuned; only someone listening to it can make the fine adjustments necessary to do this. What it means in the end is that using a tone meter does not absolve the tuner from the duty of learning his craft and fully understanding its principles. If it did, most tuners would automatically use a tone meter both for speed and for accuracy. What really matters is how the instrument sounds after it has been tuned, and there seems little point in arguing about the scientific accuracy of the tuning device or system if, in the end, the instrument does not sound as well as it should. As one of the aids to accuracy, a tone meter may be very serviceable, but by itself it does not replace the listening and discriminatory skills of the tuner.

One slight word of warning at this point; it would be inadvisable, without previous tuning experience, to try setting a temperament using only the information already supplied. Reference should also be made to the chapter on tuning keyboard instruments. Musical instruments can easily be damaged, and anyone attempting to tune should know where such damage is likely to occur, and take the necessary precautions to avoid it.

So far, only instruments with a rigid scale have been dealt with. Tempering is quite different on instruments which are completely alterable. Taking the violin as an example, in practice as well as in theory, once the four strings of the instrument have been tuned, the only *fixed* note must be that of the lowest string. Every other note can be made by the player. For anyone not conversant with stringed instruments, some explanation may be needed. The strings on a violin are tuned a pure perfect fifth apart. Beginning with the lowest string, these notes are, g, d', a' and e''. Having tuned each of these strings in relation to the others, without beats (it is usual to start from pitch a'), the lowest note, g, can only be played on the open (unfingered) g string. The other notes on the instruments are all playable without using another open string; they can all be produced from fingered positions of one or more of the strings, and some of them can be produced in a variety of different ways. Not only is it possible to produce notes without using open strings, it is in most circumstances desirable to do so.

Along with this vast degree of choice in the hand of the performer comes also the responsibility of selecting exactly the correct pitch for each and every note. Acoustically true intervals are in proportion to the fundamental note of the chord or scale which forms the harmonic basis of the music, but difficulties arise because notes produced by the correct proportions in one scale differ from notes of the same name produced proportionally from a different scale or fundamental. These difficulties are enlarged by the fact that even within the same scale, semitones and tones can be of different sizes. Since a violinist can produce acoustically correct intervals from any given note, and can do so whatever changes of key may be encountered, the rigid scale would appear to be entirely removed. The ability to play pure intervals, always in tune, whatever the circumstances, seems to be available without restriction.

Such dreams are usually short lived. In discussing keyboard temperaments, it became clear that major thirds can only be pure when combined with narrow perfect fifths or, conversely, perfect fifths can only be pure when combined with wide major thirds, when these intervals are used within the usual scales. The question now being posed is, what happens to scales and chords if acoustically correct intervals are used? The answer is that either there are some very awkward moments of intonation, or the pitch of the music appears to slide or lurch about because the implied fundamental, to which, unconsciously, both performer and listener make reference, will be constantly changing. A visual representation, in musical notation and cent values, of what can happen is given in Example 7.

The first difficulty is in assessing what is acoustically correct. Example 7 moves, as indicated, from C major through G major and then back again to C major. A string player will begin to make the journey towards the new key immediately the 'sign posts' for it have been encountered. Consequently, thinking in acoustically correct intervals depends on changing fundamentals, coupled with the variations in the series which depend on them. Since, in musical notation, only seven different note names are available, each one being alterable by means of a sharp or flat sign, no two different series can possibly run together, except over very short distances, without coming into conflict with each other.

In a passage in two parts, acoustically correct intervals must be taken into account between the parts as well as in the melody of each. This adds another dimension, that of harmony, a dimension in which the beating of mistuned harmonics will play an important part. Harmonics, being in pure relationship to the note from which they emanate, can quickly come into conflict with those produced by any note other than their own fundamental, even though the two fundamentals belong to the same scale.

In considering Example 7, certain assumptions must be made about the intervals and their relationships if any account of how the instrument might be tuned in practice is to be given. As far as the melodies are concerned (some figures for which are given above or below the squared brackets joining each note in the example), these assumptions are:

1   Thirds, fourths, fifths and octaves are constant factors if they are pure. Major thirds are 386 cents, minor thirds 316 cents, perfect fourths 498 cents, perfect fifths 702 cents and octaves 1200 cents.

2   Tones vary in size, and are greater or lesser tones of 204 cents

and 182 cents respectively, the lesser tones appearing between notes 1 and 2, and 5 and 6 of each scale.

3 Semitones vary also, but only the diatonic semitone of 112 cents is required.

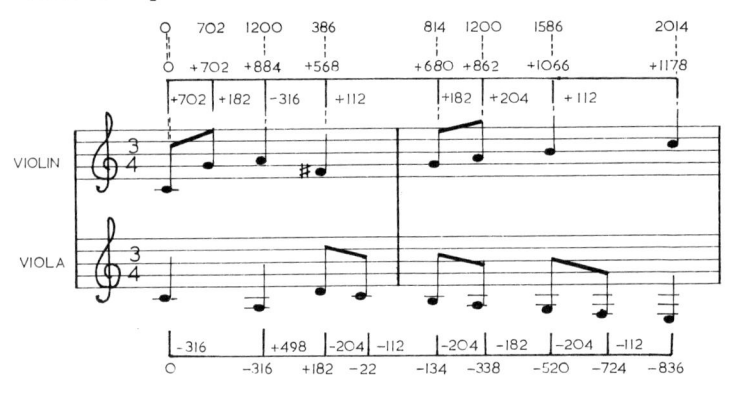

Example 7 The figures in the square brackets show the melodic movement in cents; plus means up and minus down. The figures outside the brackets show the cent value of each note in relation to a cent value c' equals O. The figures joined to notes by dotted lines give the number of cents for each interval

Turning our attention to Example 7 itself, in the violin melody, if the intervals used are those as stated above and the moves towards G major and then back to C major are taken into account, the second g' (bar 2 beat 1) will be a full syntonic comma of 22 cents, lower in pitch than the g' in the first bar. The final note, c'', will also be a syntonic comma short of a true octave above the starting note c'. In short, the pitch of the whole extract will have dropped by 22 cents in this short passage.

In the viola part something similar will happen. Within the first bar, if the first two intervals are acoustically correct, and the movement towards G major begins where marked, the first c' and the last c' in the first bar must differ by a syntonic comma, and the note a (bar 2 beat 1) will be a syntonic comma lower than the note a in bar 1 beat 2.

The harmonic implications are shown by the top set of figures. The last two intervals, of 1586 cents and 2014 cents, turn out to be true compound intervals; the first is a compound major third (1200 cents plus 386 cents) and the second, a compound minor sixth (1200 cents plus 814 cents), which means that every struck interval in the passage is acoustically correct.

Acoustically correct or not, it seems inconceivable that within the space of one bar a viola player would allow the general pitch to fall by as much as 22 cents. Although the drop in pitch is not noticeable until the beginning of bar 2 in the violin part, being obscured by the sharpened f' at the end of bar 1, the distance between the offending notes is the same in each part, namely two and a half beats. The question is, what would actually happen under such circumstances? The most likely answer is that the c', g' and a' notes will be kept at the same pitch throughout, the pitch memory of the performer ensuring this. The unisons and octaves in the passage would be kept pure. The rest of the notes will then be tempered to suit these requirements. The a' in the violin part will be slightly sharp, making the viola play a tempered minor third by raising the pitch of the note a to keep the octave good. The violinist, remembering the pitch of the first g', will keep the f' sharp as sharp as possible to make a good leading note to the g' which begins the second bar, which would involve tempering the minor third a' to f' sharp. Against this f' sharp, the viola player must raise the d', but probably the major third, d' to f' sharp, will be wider than true, stretched by the pull of the upper note as the leading note of G major and the lower note moving on next to the subdominant of G major. Although the c' in the viola part, last note in bar 1, will remain at a similar pitch to the c' at the opening, since it is only a passing note not essential to the harmony, it could, without detriment, differ slightly in pitch from the original c'. The first interval in bar 2, b to g', may well be slightly narrow, to allow the parts to stride firmly away from each other, in contrary motion to the b' in the violin part and to the f in the viola part, keeping the octave, $a - a'$, reasonably pure on the way, and slightly stretching the compound third $g - b'$. The movement towards the final note in each part may well be kept narrow, the violin b' forming a good leading note to c'', and the viola f forming a good 'leaning' note (subdominant) falling gently to the mediant of the chord of C major.

Neither player would think mathematically during these processes, nor would they aim to make the intervals exactly beatless or to make them beat at a precise speed. In the act of playing music there is no time to count beats! Beats, however, are a physical sensation; they are felt as well as heard, and although there is no time to count them exactly, there is sufficient time to make judgements about the appropriateness of their speed. A player may not aim to play an interval exactly five or ten beats per second out of tune, but would react immediately if the beat rate felt too fast. This does not mean that a player will automatically eliminate all beating. Firstly, this would be impossible, and secondly, it would probably be undesirable; judiciously controlled beating will add excitement.

This form of tempering will be achieved with great subtlety, and thereby obtain the maximum expressive effect. The soothing, gentle quality of still or slow beating chords can be contrasted with those of a faster beat, the more important or more sustained harmonies being held with a slow beat so that they do not feel to be out of tune, while the quicker beating harmonies lead with more urgency to points of climax or repose.

The effect of rigid and flexible temperaments on the playing of the same piece of music is also of interest; a comparison has therefore been attempted based on a short extract from a keyboard work by Byrd. The passage, Example 8, has a special effect in the only complete bar, a false relation between the held g' sharp in the upper part and the g natural in the lower.

Example 8 From *My Ladye Nevells Booke,* piece No 7 *A Galliard Gigge*

If played on instruments with flexible pitch, the g' sharp in the uppermost part would probably be kept as close as possible to the a' which follows it, while the g natural in the lowest part would be kept close to the f sharp which precedes it. This stretches the $g - g'$ sharp interval as far as is tolerable, but at the same time keeps the E major chord reasonably good. The fine placing of the g' sharp in relation to its functions as the major third of the chord of E major and the leading note to a' can be accomplished with the minimum detriment to either function. The note is tuned to suit the particular circumstance. The g natural in the lowest part has only melodic significance in its own line, so 'placing' it close to the f sharp will help to bind the melodic movement and help beating which would result from making the notes just. The result is more like a true diatonic than a true chromatic semitone.

If the passage were to be played on an equally tempered instrument, the g' sharp being nearer to a' than is a true g' sharp, makes it similar to the tempered g' sharp mentioned in the last paragraph. But the freedom to 'place' it in the best position for both its functions is lost. The g natural in the lowest part is closer to the f sharp than is a just g natural, so this note too approaches the position of the well-placed g natural of flexible intonation, but since the equal tempered f sharp is sharper than just, this has the effect of narrowing the g to g' sharp interval just a little from what might have been expected. However, even with this slight amount of narrowing, the g to g' sharp interval must, in equal temperament, be wider than true since the major third is wide and the minor third is narrow. The interval will therefore be stretched by the temperament, but not so accurately as it would be with the flexible instruments.

Meantone temperament would come off worst so far as any softening effect of the false relation is concerned. In ¼-comma, the g' sharp forms a just major third with the low e, while the g natural makes a slightly flat minor third with it. Consequently, the g to g' sharp interval is stretched very slightly by the temperament, but not so much as in the two cases already described.

But this is not the complete picture when discussing the bar in question. So far, only the distance between the g natural and the g' sharp has been considered, that is, the special effect of the bar. The harmonic basis is E major. In circumstances of flexible intonation, this chord can be held true, or very nearly true, erring slightly perhaps because of the pull of the A major chord in the next bar. In ¼-comma meantone, the E major chord is almost true (only the fifth being slightly narrow), but in equal temperament the chord suffers both from the slightly narrow fifth and the very sharp major third.

To sum up, flexible intonation is the most finely controlled, keeps the harmonic basis as pure as need be, while allowing for the effect of the g' sharp acting as a leading note to a'. It allows also for attention to be given to the flowing melodic bass line and the artistic handling of the discord. Quarter-comma meantone keeps the harmonic basis more or less correct, makes the g' sharp sound rather flat as a leading note and stretches the discord very slightly. Equal temperament gives the poorest harmonic basis, a reasonable leading note and stretches the discord.

Flexible intonation, implying different parts for each note played, has the added advantage that the low *g* natural can be played with less force (possible, too, on a piano but not on a harpsichord), softening the effect of the discord further, if this were desired. Instruments other than keyboards also have the advantage of vibrato, which will reduce the harsher effects of being out of tune. Vibrato could be possible on the clavichord, although in this context it would hardly be suitable to use it.

Exact figures would not enter an instrumentalist's thinking. Making one whole tone 204 cents and the next only 182 cents would not be possible, but the feeling that the first of these needed to 'reach out' towards the note which follows, while the second needs to 'draw back', keeping close to the note being played, would certainly be present. Tempering done in this way is no doubt measurable by scientific means, in retrospect, but the decisions to temper and by how much are not worked out to the last detail before the event. Very fine adjustments in keyboard tuning may also eventually come down to feeling and judgement in a similar way, but the decision to temper is deliberately taken before hand, and most of the tempering done by calculation.

How, then, can knowing about the facts of tempering help, when at the moment of doing so on an instrument with flexible intonation the amount of tempering is not calculated exactly? The answer is twofold. Firstly, it can assist in training where specific use can be made of precise information about tuning and tempering, and secondly it can assist at the moment the decision has to be made.

In training, a study of tuning and temperament can show:

1 that only intervals are tempered; notes are tuned.
2 that the finger position, or hold, gives the required note, only within tolerable limits.
3 that on a melodic instrument the musical scale can, and should be, flexible.
4 the difference between the rigid scale of the piano (equal temperament) and the flexible scale which depends on note functions.
5 precisely, the difference between a pure and a tempered interval formed between two notes sounding simultaneously.
6 how to judge exactly, by counting beats, the amount of mistuning which exists in a tempered interval.
7 that pitch memory plays an important part in staying in tune.

8 that because consecutively sounded notes do not beat, precise amounts of mistuning in melodic intervals must be approached in a different manner from that of harmonic intervals, pitch memory and note function being the guides.
9 that the only standard pitch is a' at 440 Hertz; all other notes are relative to this depending on their function and the type of scale to which they belong. The pitch of c' at 261.62 Hertz, used in keyboard instrument tuning, is calculated in relation to a' 440 Hertz as part of an equally tempered scale; c' at 261.62 Hertz has this precise pitch only in equal temperament.
10 that a working vocabulary, based on fact, can be evolved between musicians to discuss tuning.
11 that equal temperament *only* exists on a keyboard.

At the moment of playing, a study of tuning and tempering can:

1 remind a melodic instrument player that being accompanied by a keyboard instrument means that the more natural, flexible scale must be adapted to suit equal temperament.
2 help a player to decide just how far it is reasonable to mistune any particular interval in relation to its function, or functions.
3 help a player to decide that an interval should be true, and give that player some precise means of establishing what a true interval is.
4 help a player to understand how the initial tuning of an instrument relates to being in tune during the course of the music (eg a violinist playing with an oboe player can more readily assess the restrictions of the latter instrument when deciding how far it is safe to push a particular note up or down in pitch).
5 help a player to decide on the exact musical line to take during a modulatory passage, by focusing attention on note functions as well as on those notes which pitch memory demands should remain constant in pitch.
6 help a player to decide quickly, in a moment of crisis, what course of action to take. At such a moment, the two aspects, training and decision making, are brought together. Good training will provide, from the depth of a player's knowledge, some courses of action to surface almost automatically, but the decision on which of them to take in a particular circumstance must also be the result of the application of knowledge.

Most of the discussion on melodic instruments has concerned the flexible scale and intervals which are not acoustically true. Since all mistuned intervals sounding together will cause beating, however musically justified the mistuning may be, it is fair to ask why the beating is not offensive, if done expertly on a melodic instrument, when a similar amount of mistuning on a keyboard is not so readily acceptable? The first explanation must be rigidity. Since the notes of a flexible scale can be tuned to fit the circumstances and those in a rigid scale cannot, flexible intonation can be a living entity. The more offensive aspects of mistuning can therefore be avoided by allowing intervals to beat when this is appropriate and preventing them from doing so when it is not.

Another explanation, perhaps more important, is vibrato. This is not available to most keyboard intruments, but it is a standard adornment to the tone of instruments of different genres. Its use adds an undulating quality to the sound by slight, but controlled, variations in pitch (although 'slight' is not always the most appropriate word when describing some instances, particularly vocal). It is produced by a shaking movement of the wrist and /or upper arm on stringed instruments and by variations in breath pressure (or movement of the slide) in wind instruments. However produced, the reasons for the undulations are the same, namely, the raising and lowering of the pitch of a note during its production. Because of this, it can have the effect of obscuring the exact pitch of a note, which, in the case of a single note, can give the impression of beating when no beat exists, and, in the case of intervals and chords, can blur the pitch areas where beating would occur. The pulsations act like a heart beat, varying from slow and relaxed to positively feverish. The result is gentle and soothing if the width of the vibrato (its pitch variation) is narrow and its speed fairly slow, but excitement increases as the vibrato becomes wider and faster. Excitement can also depend on pitch direction, being increased as the note is pushed on the sharp side or, alternatively, plunging the listener into the depths of despair if pushed on the flat side.

Where does all this leave the keyboard? It is quite unable to compete on similar terms. Its main forms of retaliation are its dynamic range, its percussiveness and slightly mistuned intervals, the beating of which adds some excitement to the tone quality, albeit of a mechanical sort. In the league tables of pure melody it does not rate highly, but in its harmonic abilities it scores very much better. One of the first noticeable differences when playing on a qarter-comma meantone tuned instrument is that its chords seem to lack life when compared with those of equal temperaments, because they beat so little. Once accustomed to the sweeter chords of meantone in its most usable keys, the fast beating major thirds and sixths of equal temperament sound harsh rather than lively, particularly on the organ where the notes are sustained, and on the harpsichord which is rich in harmonics. The wolf intervals too have their place, giving a uniquely strident quality, especially when compared to the general stillness of the other chords. It is on the piano alone that equal temperament is truly acceptable.

Mention of the emotional impact of vibrato, beating and purity in chords, brings to mind a short section of dialogue from an old film referring to the properties of laughing gas. By way of explanation of the cause of these properties, one character remarked, 'It is the impurities which cause the laugh', which brought the reply, 'Much the same as in our modern music-halls.' (It really was an old film!) The same holds good, in some respects, when thinking of musical sounds. An interval which is acoustically pure can be less interesting than one in which there is some dissonance. It is the impurity which causes the impact. But just as surely as the mishandling of impurities in comedy can cause offence, so it is in music, that the mishandling of harmonic impurities can cause pleasure or displeasure. It is the skilful control of these impurities which is known as being in, or out of, tune, but their composition must be known before they can be effectively controlled.

4
TUNING KEYBOARD INSTRUMENTS

Tuning a keyboard instrument of any sort is a skilled job and should not be undertaken lightly. A valuable instrument can easily be damaged by rough handling or ignorance. It is only possible to consider the specific parts of the instrument which are adjusted, or otherwise directly affected, in the tuning process, but anyone not reasonably conversant with the mechanics of the instrument they wish to tune would be well advised to consult one of the many excellent books on keyboard instruments should they be in any doubt about parts of the mechanism not explained here. In all matters relating to the handling of an instrument, gentle, steady and controlled actions will gain the best results. Force should never be applied in place of knowledge and skill.

A would-be tuner must first know the functions of those parts of the instrument which are adjusted or influenced when tuning. A drawing can help description. Figure 1 shows the general principles for all stringed keyboard instruments (except the virginals and the clavichord). Although the drawing suggests a horizontal rather than a vertical instrument, the principles remain the same. Only one string is shown. A piano, which would normally have three strings for the majority of its notes (tri-cords), two strings for its tenor register (bi-cords) and single strings in the bass, differs only in number, not in kind, from the information supplied by Figure 1.

The string is attached to the hitch pin, which is itself attached to the frame of the instrument, and after passing over two bridges (the bridge nearest to the wrest pin being referred to as the nut), it is fastened to the wrest pin. Throughout its length, the string comes indirectly into contact with three separate structural parts of the instrument: the frame, the sound-board and the wrest plank. The hitch pin forms an immovable attachment point for the string. On instruments with only one string to a note, the string is usually shaped to form an eye which

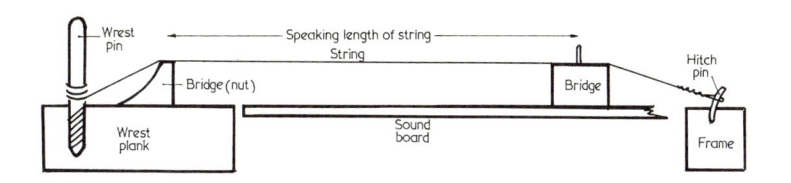

Figure 1 Details of a string

is fitted over the hitch pin. Where more than one string is needed for each note, the string is usually looped round the hitch pin, its two free ends each being fixed to a different wrest pin. In the latter case, although the hitch pin itself is immovable, the string looped round it can move as it is tightened by the wrest pins which govern it; an important consideration for the tuner.

The materials which form the frame of the instrument vary according to the type and age of the instrument. In a modern piano, the frame is metal, on an old piano and on harpsichords, spinets, virginals and clavichords, it is wood. Some harpsichords made in the late nineteenth and early twentieth centuries have metal frames similar to grand pianos, and varying amounts of metal crept into piano frames during the early nineteenth century.

The sound-board, to which at least one bridge is attached, is made of thin, straight grained wood. Since the string passes over the bridge, and by its tension presses firmly on to it, a certain amount of drag is imposed upon the string by this contact. As the string passes over the bridge, its path is deflected by one or two pins set at an angle to the string and to each other, which help to anchor the string more firmly on the bridge. Rust can occur at such contact points and inspections of them should be carried out before tuning. It is at the bridge that the maximum sound transmission from the string takes place, the sound-board accepting the vibrations of the string and, by its size and elasticity, amplifying them.

The next point of contact between the string and the main structure of the instrument is on the wrest plank. On some types of instrument there are two contact points and on others only one. Depending on design, the nut may form part of the metal frame which is attached to the wrest plank or it may be attached directly to the plank itself. In either case, the vibrations are not transmitted directly to the sound-board. In the virginals, both bridges (ie nut and bridge) are on the sound-board, but in the clavichord it is the nut which transmits sound to the sound-board; there is no bridge, as such, to do the job.

The string is finally attached to the wrest pin which is deeply embedded in the wrest plank. In modern instruments the wrest pin is drilled and the end of the string passed through the hole allowing enough string to be wrapped three or more times round the pin. In older instruments, the wrest pin is not always drilled, making the neat attachment of the string a highly skilled operation. The construction of wrest pins differs. Some are completely without threads and are gripped by the wrest plank solely because the hole into which they have been driven is slightly too narrow to accept them easily. Others are lightly threaded, mainly for ease of withdrawal, and are similarly fitted into slightly narrow holes. Some are completely threaded, the threading helping to hold the pin in place as well as allowing for easier fixing and withdrawal. In normal circumstances, it does not matter greatly to the tuner by which of these methods the wrest pin is held, since the movement of the pin necessary to make a slight adjustment to the pitch of the string is very small. It becomes critical, however, if the pin is not holding firmly in the wrest plank. The key used to tune a keyboard instrument is usually called a tuning hammer because originally the same tool was used both for hammering the pin into the wrest plank and for completing the fine tuning. Most modern tuning tools are of the lever or 'L' shape, not the original hammer or 'T' shape, and since it is the latter shape only which was used as a hammer, many tuners use the correct descriptions of lever or key when referring to the 'L' shaped and hammer for the 'T' shape. This accurate description is not, however, always observed, both the tools at times being called hammers.

If a wrest pin becomes slack, one of the methods of tightening it is to drive it deeper into the wrest plank. This method should never be used on a pin which is fully threaded. The threading of the wood inside the hole would be broken leaving the pin no grip. If a wrest pin is slack, the reason for its slackness must first be determined. There can be many such reasons, the most likely being:

1   The nature of the wood has deteriorated either through time or because there was a flaw in the original piece of wood used for the wrest plank, or because the instrument has been kept in unsatisfactory conditions.
2   The wrest plank has cracked.

3 The wrest pin has sheared at some point within the wrest plank.

Treatment of the ill must depend on its cause. If it is reason 1 above, a sharp tap on the wrest pin might be sufficient, at least for the time being if the wrest pin is not completely threaded. More drastic measures, such as removing the pin and inserting a thicker one, removing the pin and relining the hole, or using a proprietary brand of compound for expanding the wood, may be necessary. A cracked wrest plank or a sheared pin can be more troublesome. Replacing the plank is a job for an expert. Choosing suitable wood, drilling the holes to take the wrest pins and then completely restringing the instrument are not for the amateur. And calling in a professional to do the work is not always the answer either; the instrument may not be worth the cost of the repair. Drilling out the remains of a pin and fitting a new one is a much easier task, and pin extractors are available.

Broken strings are always a possibility. At best they are a nuisance, and at worst an expensive nuisance. Before attempting to tune an instrument, particularly if it has not been tuned for some time, inspect the strings for wear and rust. If either of these hazards appear, especially over bridges, great caution should be exercised. It is always safer to slacken a string first rather than to tighten it. This helps to prevent broken strings in at least three ways:

1 It allows the tuner to decide whether the string, as it stood, was sharp or flat. If it was already sharp, tightening it further may just have been enough to break it, and the unpractised ear cannot always tell immediately if a note is slightly sharp or slightly flat, even though it is obviously out of tune.

2 If, because of rust or infrequent tuning, the string has become too firmly attached to one of the bridges, adding to its tension is quite likely to break it, since more than ordinary force may be required to break the adhesion and the string, when finally freed, may move too quickly and too far. It is much safer to break such adhesions by loosening the string and making sure that it moves freely and smoothly before applying further tension to it.

3 The tuning hammer may be on the wrong wrest pin! This is not such an idiotic suggestion as it may appear. Probably more strings are broken for this reason than any other. If a slight movement of the wrest pin does not alter the pitch of the note, check the correctness of the pin before giving another turn. That extra turn might break a string if you are tightening it, or it may slacken it too much, making it less likely to stay in tune when the error has been rectified. It may also disturb the equilibrium of tension within the instrument, causing trouble with other notes.

Still concerned with wrest pins, do make sure that the tuning key fits the pin. If it does not, damage can result, restricting fine adjustments to the pin, and it is fine adjustment which ensures accurate tuning.

Tuning hammer technique
While dealing with wrest pins in general, it may be logical to continue in a similar vein, even though some of the following information is more appropriate to particular instruments. Setting a pin accurately involves the development of a good tuning hammer technique. This applies to all stringed keyboard instruments, but the actual technique may vary slightly because of the requirements of different types of instrument as well as the

Plate 1 J. Victor Pollard demonstrating the correct stance for tuning an upright piano

Plate 2 The author demonstrating a method of wrist support while tuning his harpsichord

peculiarities of individual instruments. For those who have little experience of tuning, it may be politic to make constant reference to the suggestions which follow. As with any other technique, bad habits are easy to acquire but difficult to eradicate; it is best to start in the right way even if that way does not immediately appeal or feel natural.

1 Support for wrist or arm is essential if fine adjustments are to be accurately made.
2 The tuning lever should be parallel to the direction of the string, not at right angles to it. This is most essential in tuning pianos where the tension on the string is great. When a pin is moved, it is almost certain to bend slightly, and it depends on the direction of the bending how adversely this will affect the tuning. A bent pin will eventually spring back into position, possibly altering the tension of the string and therefore the tuning. If the bending affects the lateral position of the string, unbending will simply alter the line, not the tension, of the string. If tension on the pin is applied at right angles to the string, it will tend to bend

the pin in the same direction as the string; in unbending, the tension will be altered. Holding the tuning key parallel to the string will bend the pin at right angles to the direction of the string, displacing it laterally.

3 As a further safeguard against bending the pin in the direction of the string, it is often better to stand while tuning, particularly if the resistance to the hammer is great, or if, because of the size of the instrument, it is a long reach. The more directly the tuner's power is over the pin, the less likely the pin is to bend.

4 As a corollary to suggestion three, a short hammer is often preferable to a long one.

5 The pressure applied to the hammer should be firm, but gentle.

6 It is better to move the hammer with short jerks rather than one long pull.

7 The string should always be sounding while adjustments are being made to it.

8 As well as bending, a pin is also subject to twisting. This is caused by the portion of the pin within the wrest plank staying still while the portion above the plank turns. If this happens, the note will quickly go out of tune as the pin untwists. To rectify this, the pin should be slightly 'over turned', making the note a little sharp and ensuring that the lower part of the pin has turned. The pin should then be turned anticlockwise to bring the note into tune and untwist the pin.

9 When checking the pitch of a note, do not hold the tuning hammer. It is easy to hold a note in, or out of, tune by a slight pressure of the hand, only to find that the pitch has been affected when the pressure is removed.

10 Following on from suggestion nine, take care when removing the hammer from the pin. Even this can affect the tuning on some instruments and types of instrument. Check the interval after the hammer has been removed; a simple act, but one which can save time and temper, particularly in tuning harpsichords, clavichords, virginals, spinets and old pianos.

Types of keyboard tuning

Equal temperament was a form of tuning not commonly used in England until the mid to late nineteenth century, the firm of John Broadwood & Son accepting it as standard in 1846. It had, however, been used before this time, particularly by German musicians. There is much argument about its use, but its emergence as the dominant keyboard temperament coincided with the ascendency of the piano over all other keyboard instruments except the organ. For this reason it has often been called the piano temperament.

The temperament is arrived at by dividing the Pythagorean comma, the amount by which twelve perfect fifths exceed seven octaves, equally among the fifths, flattening each one by one twelfth of a comma. Although this simple measure ensures that the series of fifths and the series of octaves then coincide, it does considerable violence to all other musically important intervals in the process. As compensation, it allows for free modulation to all keys. Making all keys equal, in this sense, removes any real feeling of 'key colour'. This somewhat controversial matter will be discussed later.

Meantone systems are concerned with the division of the syntonic, rather than the ditonic, or Pythagorean, comma. The Pythagorean comma is connected only with the fitting together of perfect fifths and octaves; major thirds only enter as by-products. In meantone systems, the quality of major thirds is part of the initial thinking, because, by definition, a syntonic comma is the interval by which a series of four pure fifths exceeds a series of two pure octaves plus a pure major third. Since the first of these two series consists of four fifths, if each fifth is diminished by one quarter of a syntonic comma, the two series will then fit together. This division of the comma gives rise to the name ¼-comma meantone − the term meantone being derived from the fact that the second degree of the scale is the exact mean between notes one and three.

The system has its limitations. These are best explained by reference to cent values. A ¼-comma meantone scale given in cent values is as follows:

C	C♭	D	E♯	E	F	F♯
0	75.5	193	310.5	386	503.5	579

G	G♯	A	B♭	B	C
696.5	772	889.5	1007	1082.5	1200

From these figures:
   A perfect fifth   is 696.5 cents
   A perfect fourth   is 503.5 cents

A major third   is 386   cents
A minor third   is 310.5 cents
A tone   is 193   cents
A diatonic semitone   is 117.5 cents
A chromatic semitone is 75.5   cents

Because there are two sizes of semitone, enharmonic equivalents cannot exist. E flat cannot be the same as D sharp, nor E sharp the same as F, and double sharps and double flats, too, are not available, as they are in equal temperament. It can be argued that since E flat and D sharp are not the same, the temperament is simply telling the truth. This may well be true, but on a keyboard, without split or extra keys, it is not possible to have both notes at one and the same time. In the tuning process it is possible to give either note, but once set, it takes at least a few minutes to make an alteration.

The scale shown above gives the usual run of notes, that is, three sharps and two flats, as well as the notes of the C major scale. In Table 2, the temperament is laid out in cent values showing the sizes of each fifth, major third and minor third. The final list in the table gives a somewhat crude, but none the less helpful, visual picture of how far out of tune certain chords are. The larger the number, the further out of tune the chord will sound.

Table 2   Description in cents of ¼-comma meantone

C	C♭	D	E♯	E	F	F♯	G
0	75.5	193	310.5	386	503.5	579	696.5

G♭	A	B♯	B
772	889.5	1007	1082.5

Fifths
C - G	696.5 (−5.5)	E - B	696.5 (−5.5)	G♯ - E♭	738.5 (+36.5)
C♯ - G♯	696.5 (−5.5)	F - C	696.5 (−5.5)	A - E	696.5 (−5.5)
D - A	696.5 (−5.5)	F♯ - C♯	696.5 (−5.5)	B♭ - F	696.5 (−5.5)
E♭ - B♭	696.5 (−5.5)	G - D	696.5 (−5.5)	B - F♯	696.5 (−5.5)

Major thirds
C - E	386	(0)	E - G♯	386	(0)	G♯ - C	428	(+42)
C♯ - F	428	(+42)	F - A	386	(0)	A - C♯	386	(0)
D - F♭	386	(0)	F♯ - B♯	428	(+42)	B♭ - D	386	(0)
E♭ - G	386	(0)	G - B	386	(0)	B - E♭	428	(+42)

Minor thirds
C - E♭	310.5 (−5.5)	E - G	310.5 (−5.5)	G♯ - B	310.5 (−5.5)
C♭ - E	310.5 (−5.5)	F - G♯	268.5 (−47.5)	A - C	310.5 (−5.5)

D – F	310.5 (–5.5)		F♯ – A	310.5 (–5.5)		B♭ – C♯	268.5 (–47.5)
E♭ – F♯	268.5 (–47.5)		G – B♭	310.5 (–5.5)		B – D	310.5 (–5.5)

Major chords

	5ths	3rds	T.
C	5.5	0	5.5
G	5.5	0	5.5
F	5.5	0	5.5
D	5.5	0	5.5
B♭	5.5	0	5.5
A	5.5	0	5.5
E♭	5.5	0	5.5
E	5.5	0	5.5
B	5.5	42	47.5
C♯	5.5	42	47.5
F♯	5.5	42	47.5
G♯	36.5	42	78.5

Minor chords

	5ths	3rds	T.
A	5.5	5.5	11
E	5.5	5.5	11
D	5.5	5.5	11
B	5.5	5.5	11
G	5.5	5.5	11
F♯	5.5	5.5	11
C	5.5	5.5	11
C♯	5.5	5.5	11
F	5.5	47.5	53
G♯	36.5	5.5	42
B♭	5.5	47.5	53
E♭	5.5	47.5	53

The figures in brackets show how far the interval is from true, either wider (+) or narrower (–). The figures for the major and minor chords show how far each of the intervals in the chord is from true, and the total gives an idea of how badly out of tune the chord will sound. Equally tempered major chords have a total of 16, and minor chords 18

An examination of Table 2 shows the following:

1 Only one perfect fifth is very much out of tune, the G sharp to E flat fifth. This is the so-called 'wolf' fifth.

2 Because of the lack of enharmonic equivalents, there are four 'wolf' major thirds, namely C sharp to F, F sharp to B flat, G sharp to C and B to E flat, all of which are wrong by a diesis.

3 For similar reasons, there are three 'wolf' minor thirds, namely E flat to F sharp, F to G sharp and B flat to C sharp.

4 Each list of chords shows eight good and four poor chords:

a) *Major Chords* All the good chords are only 5.5 cents out, because of the mis-tuned fifth. This is much better than any equally tempered major chord which is 16 cents out (14 cents for the major third and 2 cents for the perfect fifth). The four poor chords, however, are well out of tune, G sharp (or A flat) major being the worst because both the major third and the perfect fifth are mis-tuned. Of the usable chords, only E suffers as a key chord since its dominant, B major, is numbered among the poor chords.

b) *Minor Chords* Although there are only three minor thirds which are badly mis-tuned, there are still four poor minor chords, three because of the mis-tuned minor thirds, and one because of the mis-tuned fifth, G sharp to E flat. None of the chords is as badly out of tune as the G sharp (A flat) major chord, so it could appear that the minor chords do rather better than the majors. This is true of the chords in isolation, but as key chords they fare worse than the majors. Three of the four poor minor chords have good dominants (E flat, F and B flat), but four of the good minor chords have poor dominants (C sharp, E, F sharp and B). This means that the good chords, with a respectable dominant, are:

Major keys – C, D, E flat, F, G, A and B flat   (seven keys)
Minor keys – C, D, G and A   (four keys)

The general 'stillness' of the good chords in meantone is immediately noticeable when they are compared with equal temperament, but this must be balanced against the disadvantage of having some poor keys and chords. The minor keys are the worst sufferers, and even then, the above list does not show that C minor, classed as usable because it has good tonic and dominant chords and can therefore have a good perfect cadence, does not have good subdominant or submediant chords, which effectively cut out plagal and interrupted cadences.

Like equal temperament, meantone lacks key colour, except for its poor chords, the others sound similar to each other. However, the poor chords were used, at times, because, as Roger North points out, they 'by mere out-of-tuned-ness have certain characters, very serviceable to the various purposes of Musick'.

Only ¼-comma meantone has been described, but other forms of meantone have also been used, the most common being ⅕-comma, ⅙-comma, 2/7-comma and 2/9-comma.

Irregular systems are interesting for many reasons. Meantone systems produce some good and some poor chords, the good ones tending to be in those keys with small numbers of sharps or flats, but modulation is restricted because of the poor chords. In equal temperament modulation is unrestricted, but all the chords are equally, and quite a long way, out of tune. An irregular temperament seeks to keep some chords better in tune than others, but makes them all usable. In meantone and in equal temperament all the usable chords are similar in quality, but in irregular temperaments, by making some chords better than others, differing key colours can be obtained. It is true, as Roger North has pointed out, that key characteristics can exist in meantone systems, but the poorer chords are badly out of tune, whereas in irregular systems, they are not. Some irregular systems start from the assumption that C major or F major should be as good as possible, the chords becoming poorer as the number of sharps and flats increases; others, group keys together giving each group different characteristics. These characteristics are concerned solely with how close the particular chord, or group of chords, is to true. Some systems are modifications of established regular temperaments. One common modification is to split the 'wolf' in a meantone tempering between two fifths, usually accomplished by raising the G sharp to do rough service either as G sharp or A flat. Others attempt to distribute the ditonic comma (the comma of Pythagoras) in various ways. One of the most interesting is described by Vallotti and by the English theorist Thomas Young. This is a form of ⅙-comma tempering, but the comma in this case is not the syntonic comma of 22 cents, but the ditonic comma of 24 cents. The comma is distributed over six perfect fifths, narrowing each of them by 4 cents, the remaining six fifths being tuned true. Vallotti and Thomas Young differ only in the selection of fifths to be tempered, Vallotti favouring F – C, C – G, G – D, D – A, A – E and E – B, while Thomas Young in his temperament No 2 favours C – G, G – D, D – A, A – E, E – B and B – F sharp. This method gives four distinct key qualities in major and five in minor keys. An even more ingenious method is suggested by Thomas Young in his temperament No 1, giving six key colours in major and seven in minor keys. The Werckmeister temperaments also give a variety of key colours as do those by Marpurg, Neidhardt and others, and it is probable that the ⅙-comma temperament of Silbermann was ⅙ of a ditonic rather than a syntonic comma.

Requirements for particular instruments

Not all keyboard instruments have the same requirements in the tuning process. Although the differences arise from the same origin – construction – they show themselves in different ways. As well as differences, there are similarities, some of which, regarding hammer technique and sensible precautions, have been stated, but others are to do with the order of tuning known as 'laying the bearings' or 'setting the scale'. This operation is common to all keyboard instruments; an outline of it is given first, divided into steps and checks. It is intended for beginners or those who have had little experience of tuning, and has been condensed so that the important stages can be assimilated as quickly as possible without confusion or sidetracking. However, if the initial scale is to be accurately set, there must be checks to make the detection of errors easy and prevent, if possible, the annoying situation of finding that the final interval, which should close the cycle of tuning, is not correct.

Alexander Pope's line, 'To err is human', will come to mind many times in the initial attempts at keyboard tuning, and not infrequently in later attempts too. A good tuner builds a personal scheme of checks to stop errors before they start. In a cumulative process like tuning, an error, once made, can be compounded by succeeeding steps. It is therefore essential to have a pattern of tuning and checking, and stick to it, at least until some proficiency and understanding have been acquired. The important steps, with a minimum of checks, are given below. The sequence in which the notes should be tuned is arguable. Every tuner can produce good reasons to prove that his method is the best. This must be so, otherwise he would use another! But the fact that variety exists shows the arbitrary nature of the sequences, and can be confusing to a beginner. No doubt the sequence chosen here will have its detractors, but, like every other well-considered system, it will work.

Setting the scale (or laying the bearings)
The aim is to construct at least one complete octave of the temperament somewhere near the middle of the keyboard. The harmonics to listen for can be clearly heard from this area. Once the scale has been set, the rest of the keyboard is tuned in octaves. The instruction 'isolate a string' is used frequently. On some types of instrument there is only one string to a note; on others there may be two or three. If there is only one string, as on a harpsichord, no problem exists, but where there are two or more strings for a note, each must be tuned separately. To do this, the strings need to be isolated from each other with a wedge, details of which will be given later. One string is then tuned, and the others brought successively into tune with it.

The tuning sequence is given first in staff notation. The note to be tuned is shown as a semibreve, the note from which it is to be tuned is shown as a crotchet without a stem, and the pitch at which the harmonics of each note should be checked is shown, in brackets, as a guide. When checking major thirds, the beat rate

TUNING KEYBOARD INSTRUMENTS 77

will exceed the fastest metronome setting of 208. These beat rates have therefore been given in the following fashion, 'twice a metronome setting of 155' or 'three times a metronome setting of 155'. In the first of these instances there will be two beats for every single pulsation of the metronome, and in the second case three beats. The beat rates mentioned would, in fact, be equivalent to metronome settings of 310 and 465 respectively.

A slow beat can be just as troublesome as a very fast beat. If the metronome setting is less than 60, it might be more accurate to double the metronome setting and take the beat rate from each alternate swing of the metronome. If the metronome is fitted with a bell, a beat rate of 40 beats per minute (that is, a metronome setting of 40) might be more accurately established by setting the metronome to 80 and the bell to two, and take the beat rate from the ringing of the bell.

Finally, although in equal temperament the fifths are narrow and the fourths wide, in the tuning sequence given, all adjustments to notes are to be made downwards. This is possible because all the fifths are set above the note from which they tuned, so that making them narrow means tuning the upper note down slightly, whereas all the fourths are set below the note from which they are tuned so that making them wider involves tuning the *lower* note down slightly. Making all the adjustments in the same direction helps to avoid confusion, but it is not always the most satisfactory arrangement.

Step 1 Strike note c'', isolate one string, check the pitch of this one string against the tuning fork. If it beats, bring the string exactly in tune with the fork. When this has been done, alter the position of the wedge to allow one more string to vibrate and bring this string into unison with the one previously tuned. Remove the wedge entirely and bring the final string into unison. When all three strings are exactly in tune with each other, proceed to step 2.

Step 2 Having completed step 1 satisfactorily, strike note c', isolate one string and tune it as a pure octave below c'', making sure that the first harmonic of c' and the note c'' coincide exactly. Then tune the remaining strings for c' as exact unisons with the first.

Step 3 Isolate one string of note g', strike notes c' and g' simultaneously and listen for beating at pitch g''. If there are any beats adjust g' until the beating stops. Still dealing only with one string at pitch g', strike the fifth $c' - g'$ again, having set the metronome to 53, and tune g' *down* slightly until the beating at g'' coincides with the pulse set by the metronome. Remove all pressure from the tuning key and check the interval again with the metronome. When the beating is correct, tune the other strings for g' as exact unisons with the first. When all strings are tuned, check the $c' - g'$ interval again with the metronome to see that it still beats at the correct speed.

Step 4 Isolate one string for note g and strike the octave $g - g'$. By adjusting note g, remove all beating at pitch g' to ensure that the octave is pure. Tune the unisons of note g, and when they are all tuned, check again that the octave is still pure.

Step 5 Isolate one string of note d' and strike the fifth $g - d'$. Listen for the harmonic at pitch d'' and by removing all beats at this pitch, make the fifth $g - d'$ pure. Set the metronome to 40 and tune d' *down* slightly until the beating at pitch d'' coincides with the pulse set by the metronome. When this beat is correct, tune the other strings of d' as exact unisons with the first. Check the $g - d'$ interval again to see that it still beats at the correct speed.

Step 6 Isolate one string of note a, and strike the fourth $a - d'$. Listen for the harmonics at pitch a'' and by removing all beats at this pitch, make the $a - d'$ fourth pure. Set the metronome to 60 and tune note a *down* slightly until the beating at pitch a'' coincides with the metronome. When the beat is correct, tune the other strings of note a and then check that the beat rate is still correct.

Step 7 Isolate one string of note e' and strike the fifth $a - e'$. Listen for the harmonics at pitch e'' and by removing all beats at this pitch, make the $a - e'$ fifth pure. Set the metronome to 45 and tune note e' *down* slightly until the beating at e'' coincides with the metronome. When the beating is correct, tune the unisons and check the interval with the metronome as before.

Step 8: first check. Now check the major third $c' - e'$, it should beat, at pitch e''' at a speed of 20.76 beats in two seconds. This is difficult to hear. Tune down a pure octave from c' to c, and from e' to e. The beating caused by this equally tempered third can now be heard at pitch e'' and should be at a rate of twice a metronome setting of 155. If this third is not beating at the correct rate, check back over the work already done to find the error. Only when the beating of this third is correct is it safe to proceed to the next step.

Step 9 Isolate one string of note b and strike the fourth $b - e'$.

Listen for the harmonics at pitch b'' and by removing all beating at this pitch, tune the fourth pure. Set the metronome at 67 and tune note b *down* slightly until the beating at b'' coincides with the metronome. When the beating is correct, tune the unisons and check the interval with the metronome, as before.

Step 10: second check. Check the major third $g - b$, which should beat at pitch b'' at a speed of 15.55 beats in two seconds; this is a beat rate of three times a metronome speed of 155. If the first check was accurate and this is not, either step 9 or the estimating of the beat rate in this check must be wrong.

Step 11 Isolate one string of note f' sharp and strike the fifth $b - f'$ sharp. Listen for the harmonics at pitch f''' sharp, and by removing all beats at this pitch, make the fifth $b - f'$ sharp, pure. Set the metronome at 50 and tune note f' sharp *down* slightly until the beating at f''' sharp coincides with the metronome. When the beating is correct, tune the unisons and check the interval again with the metronome as before.

Step 12: third check. Check the major third $d' - f'$ sharp; it should beat at pitch f''' sharp at a speed of 23.3 beats in two seconds. Tune each note down a pure octave to notes d and f sharp respectively. The beating between these notes will now be at pitch f'' sharp, and should be at a rate of twice a metronome setting of 175. If the second check was accurate and this is not, either step 11 or the estimating of the beat rate in this check must be wrong.

Step 13 Isolate one string of note c' sharp and strike the fifth f sharp – c' sharp. Listen for the harmonics at pitch c'' sharp, and by removing all the beats at this pitch, make the fifth pure. Set the metronome at 75, tune c' sharp *down* slightly to coincide with a beat rate of half the metronome speed (the equivalent of a true metronome setting of 37.5). When the beating is correct, tune the unisons and check the interval again with the metronome, as before.

Step 14: fourth check. Check the major third $a - c'$ sharp, it should beat at pitch c''' sharp at a speed of 17.46 beats in two seconds. Tune each note down a pure octave to notes A and c sharp respectively. The beating should now be at pitch c'' sharp, and should be at a rate of three times a metronome setting of 131. If the third check was accurate and this is not, either step 13 or the estimating of the beat rate in this check must be wrong.

Step 15 Isolate one string of note g sharp and strike the fourth g sharp – c' sharp. Listen for the harmonics at pitch g'' sharp, and by removing all beats at this pitch, make the fourth pure. Set the metronome at 56 and tune note g sharp *down* slightly until the beating at pitch g'' sharp coincides with the metronome. When the beating is correct, tune the unisons and check the interval with the metronome as before.

Step 16: fifth check. Check the major third $e - g$ sharp. Note e will already have been tuned correctly for the first check, but try the octave $e - e'$ just to be sure. The major third should beat at pitch g'' sharp, at a speed of 13.08 beats in two seconds, which is equivalent to twice a metronome setting of 196. If the fourth check was accurate and this is not, either step 15 or the estimating of the beat rate in this check must be wrong.

Step 17 Isolate one string of note e' flat (d' sharp), and strike the 'fifth' g sharp – e' flat. Listen for the harmonics at pitch e'' flat, and by removing all beats at this pitch, make the 'fifth' pure. Set the metronome at 42 and tune note e' flat *down* slightly until the beating at e'' flat, coincides with the metronome. When the beating is correct, tune the unisons and check the interval with the metronome as before.

Step 18: sixth check. Check the major third $b - e'$ flat. It should beat at pitch e''' flat at 19.6 beats in two seconds. Tune each note down an octave to notes B and e flat respectively. The beating now will be at pitch e'' flat, and should be at a rate of twice a metronome setting of 147. If the fifth check was accurate and this is not, either step 17 or the estimating of the beat rate in this check must be wrong.

Step 19 Isolate one string of note b flat and strike the fourth b flat $- e'$ flat. Listen for the harmonics as pitch b'' flat, and tune note b flat to remove all beating at that pitch, making the fourth pure. Set the metronome at 63 and tune note b flat *down* slightly until the beating at b'' flat coincides with the metronome. When the beating is correct, tune the unisons and check the interval again with the metronome as before.

Step 20: seventh check. Check the major third f sharp $- b$ flat. It should beat at pitch b'' flat at a speed of 14.68 beats in two seconds, equivalent to three times a metronome setting of 147. If the sixth check is accurate and this is not, either step 19 or the estimating of the beat rate in this check must be wrong.

Step 21 Isolate one string of note f' and strike the fifth b flat $- f'$. Listen for the harmonics at pitch f'' and tune note f' to remove all beats at that pitch, making the fifth pure. Set the metronome at 47, and tune note f' *down* slightly until the beating at f'' coincides with the metronome. When the beating is correct, tune the unisons and check the interval with the metronome again as before.

Step 22: eighth check. Check the major third c' sharp $- f'$. It should beat at pitch f''' at 22 beats in two seconds. Tune each note down a pure octave to c sharp and f, respectively. The beating will now be at pitch f'' at a rate of twice a metronome setting of 165. If the seventh check was accurate and this is not, either step 21 or the estimating of the beat rate in this check must be wrong.

Step 23: ninth check. Check the fourth $c' - f'$. it should beat at pitch c''' at a rate equivalent to a metronome setting of 71.

Having completed the ninth check, tune down a pure octave from f' to f and also a pure octave from b flat to B flat. There is now a complete chromatic scale stretching from A to g'. All that remains to be done, is to tune the rest of the instrument, in octaves, from notes already set starting with the bass first.

To facilitate reading, the steps can be summarised in a similar fashion to those for ¼-comma meantone on page 52. Care must be taken over the size of the interval. The term 'narrow' does not only mean that the upper note could be flattened, it can also mean that the lower note should be sharpened. Similarly the term 'wide' can be accommodated by either sharpening the upper note or flattening the lower.

A summary of steps in tuning equal temperament:

Step		Interval	Size	Beats/sec	Metronome
1	tune	c''	true	0	—
2	tune	$c'' - c'$	true	0	—
3	tune	$c' - g'$	narrow	.8843	53
4	tune	$g' - g$	true	0	—
5	tune	$g - d'$	narrow	.66248	40
6	tune	$a - d'$	wide	.99444	60
7	tune	$a - e'$	narrow	.7436	45
8	check 1	$c - e$	wide	5.19068	2×155
9	tune	$b - e'$	wide	1.11624	67
10	check 2	$g - b$	wide	7.7772	3×155
11	tune	$b - f\sharp'$	narrow	.83468	50
12	check 3	$d - f\sharp$	wide	5.82636	2×175
13	tune	$f\sharp - c\sharp'$	narrow	.6253	37.5
14	check 4	$A - c\sharp$	wide	4.36484	2×131
15	tune	$c\sharp' - g\sharp$	wide	.93864	56
16	check 5	$e - g\sharp$	wide	6.53988	2×196
17	tune	$g\sharp - e\flat'$	narrow	.70188	42
18	check 6	$B - e\flat$	wide	4.89936	2×147
19	tune	$b\flat - e\flat'$	wide	1.05356	63
20	check 7	$f\sharp - b\flat$	wide	7.34076	3×147
21	tune	$b\flat - f'$	narrow	.78782	47
22	check 8	$c\sharp - f$	wide	5.49936	2×165
23	check 9	$f' - c'$	wide	1.1826	71

Similar details for other temperaments are given in the appendix. Equal temperament is suitable for most keyboard instruments, but meantone or irregular systems may be more appropriate at times. It would be folly to set ¼-comma meantone on a modern piano. It would not only harm the instrument, if it was being constantly altered, but also be an anachronism. Irregular systems and ⅕-comma meantone plus its variants (such as the sharpened G sharp or the Hawkes Modified ⅕-comma temperament) most certainly would have been applied to pianos and organs, especially in England, in the late eighteenth and early nineteenth centuries, and these temperaments persisted on organs until very late in the nineteenth century.

The special needs of particular keyboard instruments now require consideration.

The piano
The tools required for tuning are:

1 A tuning fork, giving c'' at standard pitch of 523.24 Hertz.
2 A tuning key, preferably an 'L' lever with a star head which fits the wrest pins of the instrument exactly. A star head enables the lever to be more easily placed in line with the direction of the string.
3 A wedge to enable the strings being tuned to be isolated from each other.
4 A metronome.

Some explanation of items three and four are needed. Taking four first, a metronome is required only if the method of tuning described above is being used. Most tuners will know the beat rate for important intervals at various pitches for equal temperament without recourse to a metronome or any of the modern electronic aids. However, if a variety of temperaments is to be set, the use of a metronome makes setting easier and more accurate.

Wedges are important. They are usually single and applied only to the group of strings associated with the note being tuned. Much of the piano is strung in tri-cords. Since, when a piano is in need of tuning, the three strings may well be at slightly different pitches from each other, it is difficult, except for a skilled tuner, to bring them into tune in any other way than separately. For this reason a simple wedge, applied first between two of the three strings to be tuned, allowing one to be free for tuning, then moved to bring in the other strings separately, is essential. Another method of wedging is to use a continuous strip of felt inserted between two of the three strings, leaving the other one free to vibrate. This is done for all the notes in the middle and upper registers of the keyboard, and the scale is set without removing this continuous wedge. This means that the scale is set only on one string of each note, and its accuracy can be checked before the wedge is progressively removed and the rest of the notes brought into tune. It is possible to construct a suitable type of wedge, but specially designed wedges, such as the Papps spring wedge, are available.

Before an attempt is made to tune a piano, it is essential that the warnings and safeguards suggested at the beginning of this chapter and the general principles described in Chapters 1, 2 and

3 have been read and understood. To these warnings and principles a few more suggestions directly relating to pianos must be added:

1 While tuning a piano, the note should be struck very firmly, much more so than it is likely to be during performance. This helps to bring to notice, as well as to even out, some of the irregularities in the string caused by twisted, bent or loose pins, or by strings being held by rust, and allows these to be rectified during tuning rather than leaving them to come to light when the piano is played loudly after tuning.

2 There are various forms, built into the piano between the wrest pin and the nut, of applying pressure to keep the string secure on the nut. These points should be inspected closely for rust or wear before the piano is tuned.

3 Take care with the wrapped bass strings, which are costly to replace if broken. They are not always available 'off the shelf', even at specialised shops, and usually have to be made to order.

4 It is always good sense first to practise tuning skills on a piano which is of little value. Having to call in a tuner to make a much used piano playable again could be embarrassing!

The information given is intended to be helpful, not daunting. It would be folly to expect perfect results at a first attempt. Although the figures and instructions given will produce correct tunings, determination, practice and discrimination are necessary too.

Early pianos

In general, all that has been said about keyboard instruments, and about pianos in particular, applies to early pianos. The term early piano is used here to mean those instruments which are entirely wooden-framed, or have only a small amount of metal bracing in their structure. They may be squares, grands or uprights, and can date from the late eighteenth century. Many of these early instruments are valuable. Find out about any particular instrument before trying to tune it. Like other stringed instruments made of wood, they are more subject to the vagaries of humidity than are modern instruments, but they can hold their tune surprisingly well in good conditions.

Since the wrest pins have oblong heads, the modern type of tuning key is not suitable. A correctly shaped key, usually a 'T' hammer, must be used. The wrest pins are not always drilled, so take special care not to break a string. Fitting a new string round a wrest pin with no hole in it, and getting it to grip, can be exasperating. Compared with a modern piano, the tuning pins need little pressure. Ease of turning, coupled with the finer gauge of wire used in these instruments generally and the softer brass wire used in the tenor register, tend to make broken strings more likely than on modern pianos.

The rest of the tuning process is the same as for a modern instrument, but it would not be out of place to use another form of tuning than equal temperament if so desired.

The harpsichord

The tension on harpsichord strings is much less than that on a modern piano, the strings themselves are much finer and there is only one string to each pitch in a particular sound colour. This latter statement is not intended to imply that there is only one string for each note on the keyboard. On a single manual instrument with two eight foot tone colours and a four foot stop, there must be at least two strings, and possibly three, to tune for each note on the keyboard. Because of this the stringing and layout of the wrest pins may appear complicated. It is therefore of the utmost importance to remember:

1 To decrease the tension on a string before increasing it.
2 To listen carefully to make sure that a decrease in tension is matched by a decrease in pitch.
3 If it is not, to check that the tuning hammer is on the correct pin for the string you are intending to alter, before proceeding any further.

As with early pianos, the tuning hammer needs to be of the right size and shape. A hammer or key which fits a modern piano will not be suitable. Because there is little tension, the likelihood of bending or twisting pins is very remote, but the advice about leaving the tuning hammer free while checking the tuning is more important. The art of taking the hammer off the wrest pin also needs to be practised. It takes very little to alter the pitch of a note on a harpsichord; constant checking is essential.

Because of the plucking action, striking the key hard to even out the tension is inappropriate. Unless the strings are rusted there will be little need to even out the tension, and if they are rusted, reducing the tension first is an obvious precaution.

Harpsichords are rich in harmonics. Those required for tuning are easy to hear. So, unfortunately, are many others. Be sure to select those which are immediately useful and disregard the rest. Because of the greater number of harmonics, equal temperament sounds coarser on a harpsichord than on a piano. Try one of the meantone, or one of the irregular, temperaments; in any case, such temperaments are more suited to the music to be played on the instrument unless it is a modern composition.

The virginals

If the name of this instrument is derived from 'virga', Latin for 'a rod', virginals is better than virginal. Only one rod, or jack, would imply a very primitive instrument. In a similar context 'a measle' or 'a mathematic' would look and sound peculiar; in the plural, as measles and mathematics, they are much more familiar. The instrument is similar to the harpsichord and the spinet, except that both bridges are on the sound-board. The vibrations of the string are thus transmitted through both bridges exciting the sound-board in two different places simultaneously, which is one of the reasons for the distinctive sound of the instrument. Another is that the strings are plucked at or near the

Plate 3 A virginals by Dennis Woolley. The jacks, covered by the jack rail bearing the maker's name, pluck the string near to its mid-point

middle, disturbing that area of the string at which the node for the second harmonic forms. Because the second harmonic is so useful in tuning, it is imperative to listen to the single notes before striking them in pairs for tuning purposes. If the usual harmonics have been disturbed, the precise pitch of beating will need to be established. If the most audible beat rate is being formed in a different octave from that which may normally be expected, the figures suggested here may have to be multiplied by 2, 3 or even 4 to give the correct amount of tempering. Only discriminative listening can establish whether or not any accommodation of the figures is required.

In other respects the virginals is similar to the harpsichord and spinet in tuning.

The spinet

Since this is really a small harpsichord, the tuning process is similar, but there is not the complication of a large number of strings. In antique shops, square pianos are frequently referred to as spinets. There need not be any confusion between the two instruments. Apart from size, the piano usually being much bigger and heavier than the spinet, if the sound is produced by hammers striking the strings, it is a piano. A spinet has a plucking action like a harpsichord.

The clavichord

The clavichord poses different problems in tuning, because the method of sound production is unique to this instrument (see Figure 2). Vibrations are transmitted to the sound-board by the nut (that is, the bridge nearest to the wrest pin) and there is no other bridge between that and the hitch pin. When the string is at rest, its speaking length is not defined. Sound is produced by the string being struck by a brass tangent, not plucked by leather, quill or nylon plectra. If a string is struck by a soft hammer, and that hammer is left in contact with the string, vibration will be curtailed and little or no resonant sound produced. An instrument working on this principle, such as a piano, needs an escapement action to allow the hammer to fall back freely from the string, leaving the string to vibrate. In the case of the clavichord, although its sound is produced by striking the string, the mechanism of sound production, namely the tangent, actually forms the second bridge, defining the vibrating length of the string as well as causing the string to vibrate. Briefly, the

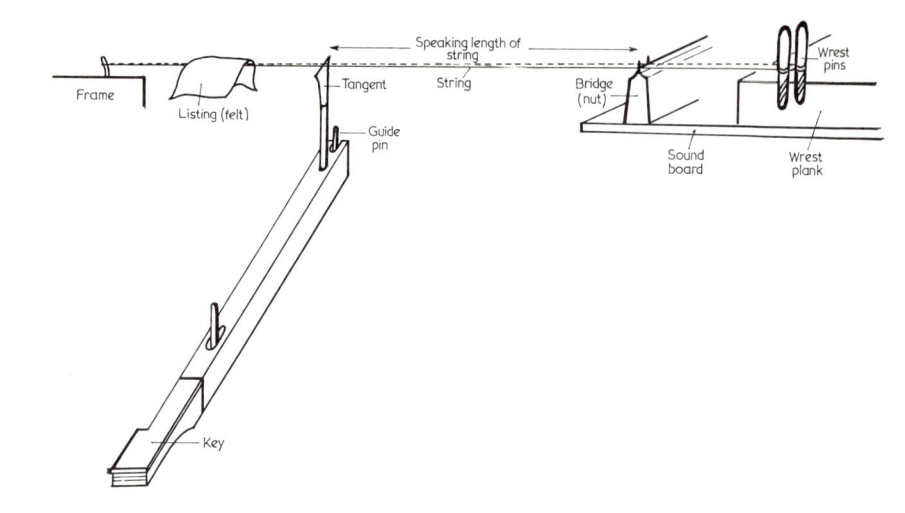

Figure 2 Details of clavichord action

mechanism is a simple lever, one end of which is shaped to form the finger key, and the other supporting, at right angles to its length, a brass rod flattened at the top to form a sharpish edge (Figure 2). When the key is depressed, the sharp edge strikes the string, causing it to vibrate while at the same time determining the speaking length. To stop the string producing two notes when divided by the tangent, the speaking length of string (that between the nut and the tangent) is left free to vibrate, and the non-speaking length (that between the tangent and the hitch pin) is deadened by a strip of felt (known as listing) woven between the strings.

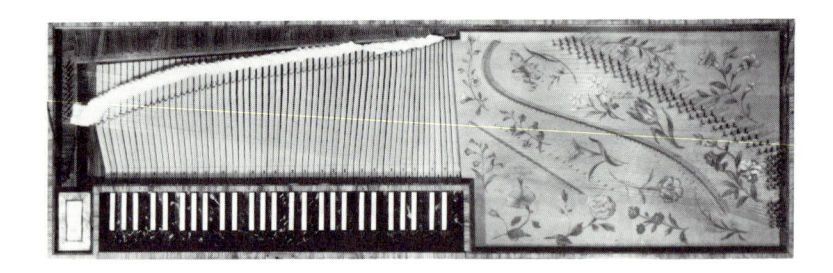

Plate 4 The J. A. Hass clavichord (1763) in the Russell Collection, St Cecilia Hall, Edinburgh, showing the listing between the hitch pin anbd the striking point of the tangent. *(Picture by permission of The Friends of St Cecilia Hall)*

Some detailed explanation of the sound production mechanism has been necessary, since it is obvious that the string, when at rest, will be at a different pitch from that of the speaking part of its length when the tangent is raised. Tuning can therefore only be done when the key is depressed and the tangent in contact with the string. There is a further complication. The pressure applied to the key influences pitch. The further the string is displaced by the tangent, the higher will be its pitch. By altering the pressure on the finger key, a vibrato can be created. This effect is known as the *Bebung* (German for 'shaking'). When tuning, therefore, a similar pressure must be exerted on each key to ensure that when the instrument is played with a constant finger pressure it will remain in tune with itself.

Since the amounts by which keyboard intervals deviate from true is small, particularly the tuning intervals of fifths and fourths, accuracy is difficult on a clavichord. But the very nature of the instrument which makes it difficult to tune also obscures the constancy of pitch during performance; what you gain on the roundabouts you lose on the swings! Such arguments can be carried too far. The instrument still needs to be tuned as accurately as possible if it is to sound well, and the principle of listening for harmonics still holds.

The organ
It is not within the scope of this book to deal with the tuning of various types of organ pipe. The beat rates given for tunings apply equally well to organ pipes as they do to strings.

Tuning to temperaments other than equal
The tendency during the twentieth century has been to give temperaments, other than equal, a cursory, historical nod and little else. Equal temperament, particularly in England, is a newcomer to the scene of instrumental tuning, and like many newcomers has distorted the historical perspective. The supporters of equal temperament argue its antiquity, dating it back, so we are told, to the ancient Chinese. No doubt the possibility had been known in principle, but little convincing explanation is given as to why, if it is such a natural and logical temperament, it was not consistently used until late in the eighteenth century on the continental mainland, and the mid-nineteenth century in England. Far from being an argument in its favour, the fact that equal temperament was known but

deliberately not used, is a strong incentive not to use it for music written before the mid-eighteenth century, and probably not for music written long after that date. For many who have not heard any other keyboard temperament but equal, the thought of having some out of tune chords appear in the music of Bach, Handel, Purcell, Couperin or of any earlier keyboard music seems intolerable. On the face of it, it is hard to defend such arguments while being content to listen to such music played on a temperament in which *every* chord is out of tune.

For those who are willing to try them, tuning schemes are given for a variety of well-known temperaments. To assist in selecting an appropriate temperament, origins, with dates and places, have been attached to each wherever possible. The schemes, and information about them and their settings, appear in the Appendix.

5
BRASS AND WOODWIND INSTRUMENTS

This chapter could be very brief. All a player can do before starting to play on a woodwind or brass instrument is move the tuning slide(s), barrel, head or reed or make whatever adjustment is appropriate until the tuning note is accurate, and the rest of the instrument will be brought into tune automatically. The fine tuning of notes is then done by the player during performance. These instruments already have a chromatic scale built into them by way of a valve system of finger holes. Only brass instruments without valves do not, and of these only the trombone has the possibility of an entirely free chromatic scale. The tuning process would appear to end when the tuning note has been fixed, but this is far from the truth of the matter. It would be more accurate to describe this as the mid-point of the process rather than its end. Before the instrument is tunable, even within limits, considerable demands have already been made on the designers and craftsmen who conceived and constructed it, and after the tuning note has been taken, the performer has, from moment to moment, to adjust the fine tuning in order to make music. The mid-point of tuning to an A or a C is hardly tuning at all in the true sense of the word. The real tuning is done in manufacture and performance; the taking of an A or C establishes a common pitch for one note only. It could well be called taking the pitch, rather than tuning.

Although taking the pitch is common to brass and woodwind instruments alike, there are differences. The pitch is best taken when the instrument is warmed up; otherwise the pitch will rise. The standard pitch is a' 440 Hertz at 68° F and as the temperature fluctuates, so will the pitch. It is only possible to alter the pitch of an instrument a small amount without disturbing the relative distances between the notes. A pitch alteration lengthens or shortens the tube in one place only; it does not alter it proportionally to the valves or finger holes already built into the instrument. Woodwinds are less flexible than brass in this respect. It would be difficult to devise a system which would alter the distance between every hole proportional to the alteration in the complete length of the pipe; all that can be done is to adjust the length of pipe near the head of the instrument. On brass instruments, there is the possibility of adjusting the extra lengths of tubing inserted for each valve as well as the general length of the instrument. But instruments are designed to play at a particular pitch, and to expect them to deviate substantially from it is asking too much. If, in order to play with an instrument of fixed pitch, like a piano or organ, on which the pitch is either higher or lower than standard, and the maximum amount of adjustment is required from a wind instrument, it is a wise precaution to check the effect that this has had on the intervals between the notes through the compass, even though the pitch of the tuning note seems to be correct.

Tuning similarities between brass and woodwind instruments

Although it is the differences rather than the similarities between the tunings of these instruments which are of greatest interest, dealing with their similarities under one heading saves repetition. Because they are melodic rather than harmonic, the tuning of any individual brass or woodwind instrument cannot be done either by counting beats or by recognising the lack of them. Beating can occur between two notes only when they are heard simultaneously, not when they are heard consecutively. It is only by comparison with another source of sound that beating can be used as a tuning test.

Both categories of instrument are governed in pitch and in the intervals between the notes of the scale within their compass by their original length and by the positioning of keys or fingerholes or the exact lengths of tubing which each valve adds to the main body of the instrument. Although the methods of changing the pitch of individual notes give some latitude, it is by no means as great as that enjoyed by entirely alterable instruments. What latitude there is is usually coupled with an alteration in tone quality. Pitch and tone quality are frequently at odds with each other. The trombone is the odd man out in that extensions to the length of tubing are minutely variable and not confined to letting in or taking out set lengths of tubing, suddenly and as complete units only. Brass instruments of the bugle type, without valves or slides, come into yet another category. Pitch, in this latter case, depends on the length of tubing, and intonation and note range on the skill of the player unassisted by standard fingering patterns.

In design, manufacture and in individual tuning at factory level, brass and woodwind instruments suffer from the difficulty that notes cannot be tuned in isolation. What may be good for the intonation of one note may upset others. As many of these problems as possible are dealt with before an instrument leaves the factory, but each solution is a compromise. The ranges, designs and qualities of instruments reflect both the materials used and the type of compromise effected between intonation and tone quality. Makers can, and do, supply instruments with modifications specified by the purchaser, although they may be reluctant to do so if the modification upsets the instrument in other ways. Instruments for general sale are supplied in specific qualities, the more expensive of them being individually tuned and finished with the needs of particular types of musician in mind. A good salesman should know the characteristics of the instruments he is selling, but in cases of doubt a reputable maufacturer will on request give details of the materials used and reasons for the differences in quality, price and performance for similar types of instrument.

A manufacturer is interested in tone quality as well as intonation, and in the needs of the professional, the student and the amateur. These interests and needs can often be in conflict. Taking only the aspect of intonation, the requirements of individuals and groups vary enormously. A beginner needs a low-priced instrument (because he may not continue to learn), which will give reasonable tone throughout a reasonable compass, which speaks readily and is easy to play in tune. Being easy to play in tune means, in this context, that the orthodox fingerings leave as little room for choice (or latitude of intonation) as possible. As choice recedes so compromise takes over. The most acceptable constant compromise is equal temperament. The instrument should therefore be able to give an equally tempered scale, with little room for manoeuvrability, and be at standard pitch. An instrument designed this way would allow young players to play together with like or dissimilar instruments, and to do so with a reasonable quality of tone, but at the same time make the minimum demands on their technique. The advantages are immediately obvious, so much so that the disadvantages may be obscured. Leaving aside any considerations of mouthpiece or reed, to a musical student of whatever age the lack of flexibility would become irksome. Although the tone quality may, with little effort, be reasonable, it will never be very good or greatly variable, and the intonation, while seldom a disaster, will equally seldom be absolutely correct. These limitations could encourage aural laziness in students who, though capable of discriminating, may become unaware of the need for, and the possibility of, being so. In short, a gifted or even an average player could quickly outgrow this type of instrument. The advice of an experienced teacher is needed in any individual circumstance, but a good student will begin to feel the restriction, while a less perceptive one may need to be told of it.

At the opposite end of the spectrum, a professional musician needs the maximum amount of latitude in both tone quality and intonation to satisfy the dictates of the music he is to play. Coupled with latitude, he needs control; control which remains in his hands, not built into the instrument. As well as being designed and tuned to give him this facility, it must do so throughout its compass. To a professional musician, tone quality, intonation and compass are concerned as much with what he can make the instrument do as they are with what it gives him for little effort.

To expect one design and quality of instrument to cover both requirements is clearly asking the impossible, and there are many shades of requirement within these extremes which are equally valid. Add this to the fact that many instruments are made from organic materials which are themselves variable, and the whole business of instrument-making begins to look like a golf course consisting solely of an infinite number of bunkers and a few very small greens.

Seeking and receiving guidance about the quality of instruments still leaves the task of choice to the purchaser. The best instruments may not be the best of choices. It could result in a situation rather akin to putting a learner driver into a Formula One racing car – the margin for error would be very great and the likelihood of immediately harnessing its potential similarly remote. However, it is always wise to buy something which does not restrict. Freedom can only be achieved by personal control and responsibility; restriction inhibits both.

Brass instruments

In the opening paragraph of this chapter, it was suggested that bringing an instrument into pitch was simply the mid-point of a tuning process which begins in the factory and ends in performance. The following quotation from an article entitled 'Systematic approach to the correction of intonation in wind instruments' appeared in the magazine *Nature* on 26 August 1976. Written by Dr Richard A. Smith of Messrs Boosey and Hawkes and Dr Geoffery J. Daniell of the Department of Physics, Southampton University, it defines the areas from which scientists involved in the design and manufacture of instruments begin to tackle the problems of intonation:

> Musical instruments have evolved over the centuries very much by trial and error. In spite of scientific investigation, many undetermined factors critically affect the performance of instruments, and empirical methods of design are still necessary. Some features, however, are easily amenable to quantative treatment, and we present here the results of some calculations and experiments on improving the intonation and tone colour of the trumpet.
>
> All brass instruments have acoustical and mechanical inadequacies for which most players automatically compensate. To the average listener an instrument may sound perfectly in tune but this is largely the competence of the player who may be able to 'lip' a note by ± 1 semitone, usually at the expense of tone colour. Similarly, the intonation of inexperienced players tend to be more affected by the deficiencies of their instruments.

Since an instrument designer is interested in the quality of sound as well as in intonation, and is dealing with actual materials, not just theories, he has to cope with the resonances of the shape on which he is working. In theory, it would appear that all would be well; they should form in the tube in proportion to the figures for pure intervals as from a fundamental note C in Example 1, page 18. In practice it is not so simple; the article points this out:

> The resonance frequencies are principally determined by the shape of the bore of the trumpet, and evolution has produced a bore shape with resonances fairly close to the appropriate notes of the equitempered scale. Unfortunately intonation is not the only consideration in fixing the resonances. . . .
>
> In practice, the harmonics of any note fall near but not exactly on the resonances of the tube, and are, to varying degrees, reinforced by resonance. The resonances strongly affect the tone colour of notes,

and hence the choice of a set of resonances is inevitably a compromise between their intonation when used as fundamentals and their reinforcement of the harmonics of other notes.

Again the word compromise appears, as it so often has already. In brass instruments it is not a compromise between the tolerable and the intolerable as it was in keyboard tuning, but between intonation and tone quality. The terms intonation and tone quality need to be discussed in this connection, when the final stage in the tuning process is reached, as well as in this, the first, stage. They are not only the responsibility of the instrument maker and designer, but he must offer an instrument with sufficient stability as well as flexibility.

Before continuing with some further information from the article, it is necessary to describe some of the parts and functions of the instruments as they affect tuning and intonation. There are various ways of classifying brass instruments, each of which has some bearing on intonation. Firstly, they are described by their bore shapes. These, not taking the flare at the bell end into consideration, are either parallel (cylindrical) or conical. Trumpets and trombones fall into the former group, while horns, cornets and other members of the brass band family fall into the latter. Explanations of why columns of air react in different ways in parallel- or conical-bore instruments can be found, as far as they are known, in books describing the physical basis of sound. In general, conical-bore instruments overblow (change mode) to even-numbered harmonics, whereas those with a parallel bore change mode to odd-numbered harmonics. Referring again to the harmonic series (p18), it would appear that a parallel pipe would not be able to produce any octaves, since these are all even-numbered harmonics. Had the parallel-bore instrument been open at both ends, like the flute, matters would be different, but it would be a great disadvantage on a brass instrument to be deprived of the facility of over blowing at the octave. But no one would deny that trumpets and trombones, both parallel-bore instruments, can be overblown at the octave. Professor Taylor, of University College, Cardiff, in *The Physics of Musical Sounds*, explains why:

> It would appear that the lips of the player form a more-or-less closed end, and one might expect that a cylindrical pipe giving only odd harmonics would not be ideally suited to an instrument based on mode-changing. Fortunately (or unfortunately!) there are complica-

tions which make the instruments satisfactory but at the same time make a clear physical understanding of their operation more difficult. In fact, the physics of the brass instruments still holds some fascinating problems which are by no means completely solved.

He also points out:

> If one bears in mind that the lips do not behave completely as a closed end, that even the trumpet becomes conical for part of its bore, and that reed or lip frequency can 'pull' the frequency of the pipe by at least a semitone from the natural frequency, it is possible to see why both the horn and the trumpet can give satisfactory sequences by mode-changing.

The second classification is between brass instruments which are restricted to one harmonic series and those which are not. The notes on all brass instruments are governed by the harmonic series, but those with valves or a slide mechanism are not confined only to the harmonic series from one fundamental. By altering the speaking length of tubing, and therefore the fundamental note, valves and slides fill the gaps inevitable in an instrument confined to the harmonic series in one position only, and allow a chromatic scale to be formed.

To lower the pitch of a brass instrument by a semitone, approximately 6 per cent of the speaking length must be added to its tubing. To lower the pitch by a further semitone would involve an additional 6 per cent of the new length of tubing, which is 6 per cent of 106 per cent of the original length. The progression is geometric not arithmetic. By letting in prescribed lengths of tubing the valve system works well so long as separate valves are being used, but since each valve lets in a specific length of tubing, not a proportionally increasing or decreasing length, troubles occur when valves are used in combination. To give a rough idea of what happens, in figures, assuming a speaking length of tubing of 147in (373.38cm), approximately the length of a modern French horn, and taking the round figure of 6 per cent as the additional amount of tubing required for each semitone, the following figures would emerge: to reduce the pitch by a semitone, 6 per cent of 147in (373.38cm) is 8.82in (22.4cm), the new length of pipe would then be 155.82in (395.75cm). To reduce the pitch by a further semitone (a full tone below the original pitch) a further length of tubing equal to 6 per cent of 155.82in (395.78cm) would be required; that is 9.34in (23.72cm). to lower the original note produced by 147in

(373.38cm) of tubing by a full tone would require the addition of 8.82in (22.4cm) plus 9.34in (23.72cm), which is 18.16in (46.12cm), making a new length of 165.16in (419.5cm). To reduce the pitch by a further semitone (three semitones, or a minor third below the original note) a further length of tubing equal to 6 per cent of 165.16in (419.5cm) would be required, that is 9.91in (25.17cm). This added to the 18.16in (46.12cm) required to lower the note by a tone, means that 28.07in (71.29cm) of tubing would have to be added to the original length of 147in (373.38cm), to lower the pitch by a minor third. The new length of tubing required to produce this note would be 175.07in (444.67cm).

Presenting these figures in terms of lowering the pitch in steps of a semitone, starting from 147in (373.38cm) of tubing, the first semitone would require 8.82in (22.4cm) of extra tubing, the second semitone would require a further 9.34in (23.72cm), and the third semitone would require a further 9.91in (25.17cm) of tubing.

On a three-valve instrument, the first valve lowers the pitch by a tone, the second by a semitone and the third lowers it by a minor third, or three semitones. If, however, the pitch were to be lowered by four semitones (a major third), using valves two and three would produce a note which is too sharp. To make the fourth semitone correct and therefore lower the original pitch by a major third, the tubing would need to be increased by 6 per cent of 175.07in (444.67cm), that is 10.5in (26.67cm), whereas the second valve would only add 8.82in (22.4cm). The true length of tubing needed to produce four semitones, or a major third, below the original pitch would be 185.57in (471.35cm) whereas valves two and three together would only produce a tube length of 183.89in (467.08cm), which is 1.68in (4.26cm) too short.

On some instruments a fourth valve is added to lower the pitch by a perfect fourth (five semitones), which when used in combination with the other valves completes the downward scale to the fundamental. The introduction of yet another length of tubing complicates matters still further if it is to be used in combination with the original three valves.

Various methods have been used to help correct these errors. Some makers supply a fifth, or even a sixth, valve to introduce extra lengths of tubing. Another system, designed by D. J. Blaikley, a well-known name in brass instrument design in the late nineteenth century, consists of compensating pistons built into the existing valves which operate when the valves are used in combination. Since the problem only exists when extra lengths of tubing need to be added, Adolphe Sax looked at the problem in an entirely different fashion, by subtracting lengths of tube; his system, which requires six valves, has not found favour.

The valves are of three different types – piston, double piston and rotary. Of the double piston, Philip Bate in the article entitled 'Valves' in *The New Grove* (Vol 19), writes:

> The Vienna valve, although once very popular with Belgian instrument makers (to the extent that it was miscalled 'système belge') is now confined almost entirely to Austrian players and their pupils, the splendid french horns of the Vienna PO setting the example.

The Vienna valve is of the double piston variety. In the usual piston valve there is a cylindrical piston working vertically in a casing. When the piston is in its normal position, the air passages through it form part of the main tubing; when it is depressed an alternative direction of air flow through an extra length of tubing is formed. The valve is depressed against a metal spring which returns it to its normal position when released. The rotary (rotary cylinder, or cylinder) valve, also controlled by a metal spring, is often described as a four-way stopcock turning in a cylindrical case. Two of the four ways form part of the main tubing and the other two, when the valve is rotated 90 degrees, allow an alternative direction of air flow through an extra length of piping. The rotary valve is more commonly used in America and on the European mainland than in England. Although it is the extra length of tubing which alters the pitch of the note, not the valve itself, the valve mechanism is crucial to correct intonation. To work efficiently, valves must be airtight. Precision ground pistons are best, since plating can vary in thickness, and the valve should be lubricated. Players often seem to have their own methods of lubrication, few of which, however, appear in the maker's recommendations!

Diameter of bore also affects intonation and tone quality. A wide bore gives greater flexibility to both. To the casual observer there would appear to be little or no difference between a wide- and a medium-bore instrument. This is hardly surprising. The difference between a large- and medium-bore cornet, for example, may be only 0.16mm (or 0.006in), but an experienced player would readily appreciate the accuracy of intonation and flexibility of tone quality that the larger bore gives.

The trombone, because of its slide mechanism, does not require valves in the same way as other brass instruments, although there are trombones which do work on the valve principle. It is the only brass instrument which comes into Bottrigari's class of entirely alterable instruments. Intonation is solely in the hand and lips of the performer. Valves can be fitted as a permanent part of the instrument or as an optional attachment. A detachable tuning slide can convert a B flat into a B flat and F instrument, with the possibility of the tuning slide pulling out to E. The bass, or tenor/bass trombone can have a two valve system, one being the conventional F valve and the other a G valve. Used together they produce E flat. The valves, although working in the same way as any other valve by allowing extra lengths of tubing to be added and removed, are needed to allow lower notes to be added to the compass, not to make the instrument chromatic.

Brass instruments without valves are showing an increase in popularity. Valves were invented in about 1813, and their history, from invention, through rejection on the grounds of tone quality and reliability, to their eventual acceptance, makes interesting reading. But brass instruments were used long before the invention of valves, and only the trombone, which did not enter the symphony orchestra until quite late because of its ecclesiastical connexions, was fully chromatic.

The two most common valveless brass instruments still in use are the bugle and the 'natural' horn. The former has a distinguished history as an instrument for signalling and for general military use. Its usual compass is from the third to the sixth harmonic. The horn, although it has become modernised and accepted valves, was used as a natural instrument in the orchestra for many years. All horn parts in the Classical period and earlier are for instruments without valves, as are many others stretching well into the Romantic period. Although the instruments are, at any moment, confined to the harmonic series from one fundamental only, that fundamental can be changed by the insertion of another crook. This is, in essence, similar to adding or removing lengths of tubing by the use of valves, but there are important differences. Re-crooking, while altering the length of tubing, still allows for the natural air flow through the instrument; valves do not. The alterations to the lengths of tubing being made by diverting the air flow round numerous, twisting wind ways affect the tone as well as the pitch, even though modern designers have eliminated sharp corners and edges to a large extent and made the air ways smoother. Although re-crooking keeps the natural brilliance of tone, it takes time and does not allow for quick chromatic changes. The lengths of crook, like the extra lengths of tubing let into the system by valves, are predetermined; the player, however, has to produce the notes, but the crook change is like a change of fingering. In about 1760 the Dresden horn player Hampel discovered that the notes of the natural horn could be lowered a semitone, or even a whole tone, by placing the hand, with fingers closed, into the bell. The immediate increase in the chromatic possibilities of the instrument was useful, but again it was gained at the expense of tone quality. The stopped notes differed in timbre from the open notes. There is still a place for this, the so-called hand horn. Just as equal temperament should not render other forms of keyboard tempering obsolete, valves should not oust natural instruments.

This discussion of brass instruments began by quoting from an article by Dr Richard A. Smith and Dr Geoffrey J. Daniell; to show the highly technical nature of solving intonation problems

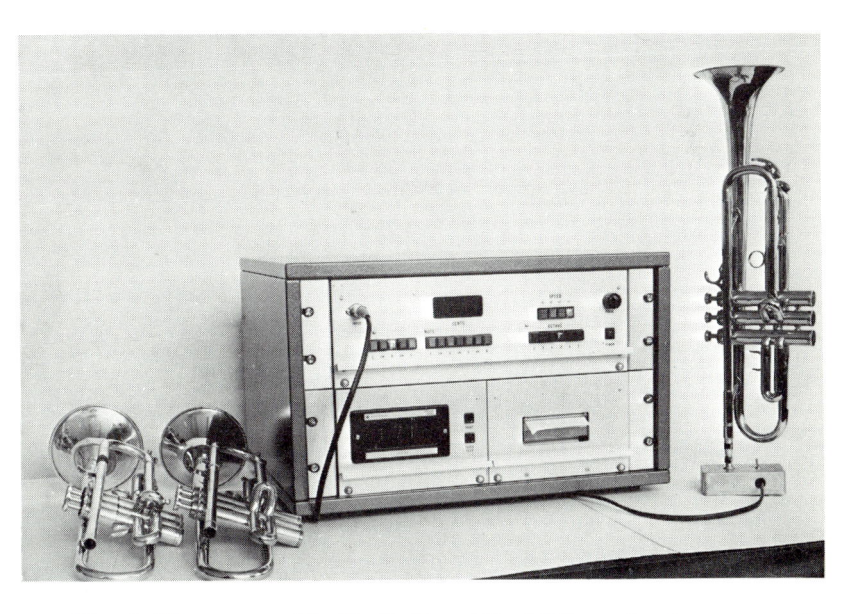

Plate 5 The tuner used by Drs Smith and Daniell for testing the accuracy of brass instruments

in brass instruments further reference will be made to it. To gain information for the article a 'trumpet was driven by an automatic tuner'. The tuner is described in the following terms:

> The apparatus [see Plate 5] . . . includes an automatic locking device for the location and tracking of resonance peaks. It gives digital display and printed record of the amplitude and intonation of each resonance (in cents) relative to the eqitempered scale.

By calculation and use of this machine a new bore shape is worked out, 'reproduced with glass reinforced plastic and its resonances measured using the automatic tuner'. The whole process is a highly technical and scientific operation, from the results of which slight alterations in bore diameter can be made to improve the intonation of any desired resonance.

This cruelly truncated version of a most interesting article has been given to show the way in which improvements in brass instruments are arrived at. Although a modification may be accompanied by slight alterations in the appearance of the instrument, it is the constant concern of designers to improve the performance of the instruments being produced. Such improvements in brass instruments are the result of detailed scientific investigation and research.

Woodwind instruments

Woodwind is not the most accurate description of instruments in this category, because many of them are no longer made of wood. Good quality clarinets, oboes, cor anglais, bassoons and recorders are still made from wood, but many cheaper instruments are of plastic. Flutes are of metal, although early instruments, and modern copies of them, are made from wood. Saxophones, usually classed as woodwind instruments, have always been made of metal, with mouth-pieces containing a single reed like that of the clarinet.

The principle of producing sound differs from that of brass instruments. Instead of relying on changes of harmonics only, the sound wave in the instrument is controlled by vents cut through the wall of the tube. These vents are closed or opened, either by the direct contact of the player's fingers or by pads operated from keys built on the surface of the tube. The vents alter the speaking length of the column of air, their position determining how that column of air is divided. The air is excited in two different fashions, edge tone and beating reed. In instruments of the flute family, the player directs a stream of air (or has it directed from him by a wind way) on to a sharp edge which divides the stream of air, causing vibrations. In the reed family there are two subdivisions, single- and double-reed instruments. On a single-reed instrument like the clarinet, the player directs a stream of air onto the reed causing it to vibrate against the mouthpiece. With a double-reed instrument like the oboe, the vibrations are caused by the beating together of two reeds, bound and shaped to form the mouthpiece of the instrument.

The stages of the tuning process are similar to those for brass instruments, taking the action by the player of setting the pitch of the instrument as the mid-point.

Beginning, as before, with the maufacturer's contribution to tuning, the general pattern, the length of instrument and the positioning of holes has been established by trial and error over many years. Plastic instruments are made in moulds, which in turn have been derived from the traditional patterns, and wooden instruments are drilled by using jigs to determine the exact position of each hole as well as its size and angle. At this stage, the instrument is drilled to accept the posts on to which the key system will be fitted as well as for the acoustically located holes. The usual key system applied to these instruments is the Boehm system. Although there are modifications applied to it by various makers, the basis remains constant.

After drilling and the fitting of the key mechanism, the instrument comes into the expert hands of a tuner. Depending on the size of the manufacturer, maker and tuner may be one and the same craftsman. Whatever the circumstances, the fine tuning stage is accomplished in a similar manner. Where necessary, the holes are undercut, by inserting a sharp cutting tool into the hole and removing a small amount of wood from the lower edge of the hole. This operation is obviously highly skilled. It demands knowledge, experience and craftsmanship, but is almost impossible to describe in words. Unlike brass instruments, on which the fine adjustments to intonation are worked out by calculation, verified by special apparatus and tested and tried on prototype instruments before the machines in the factory are fractionally altered to incorporate the new element in design, the sophisticated apparatus used in woodwind tuning is the craftsman's hand, eye and ear, coupled with his knowledge of how alterations made to one note may affect another. Such is the

Plate 6 Dave James tuning a clarinet

nature of wood, no two instruments will be exactly alike. Even a blunt drill, or a piece of wood which splinters more easily than another can have their effect at this stage.

Plate 6 shows such a craftsman at work on a clarinet. Using a tone meter to give an accurate scale, he must bring the instrument he is tuning as closely as he can to that scale, using his experience to know just when to leave the rest of the tuning to the performer.

Because these instruments are individually tuned, adjustments can be made to suit the requirements of individual artists. Since fine tuning is a compromise, it can be made to favour some notes rather than others. For instance, an artist making an important appearance, possibly in front of television cameras and an audience of millions, may, understandably, wish to ensure the accuracy of some particularly taxing passage. This would need to be done at the expense of other notes; if it were not so the instrument would be tuned that way originally. An expert tuner can accommodate the performer in this respect, and, furthermore, can restore the instrument to its former tuning by the judicious use of tuning wax or some similar material. Such refinements are unnecessary for the average player, but they are available to those whose livelihood may depend upon them.

There have been some significant developments recently in woodwind design, two of which at least are worthy of mention. The first concerns the clarinet, and is a vent F sharp mechanism. It is claimed that the improvement produced by this mechanism 'is not one of facility alone, as is so often the case with new mechanisms, it is an improvement of the essential acoustics of the instrument — one of the few which have been made since the days of Klosé and the introduction of the so called Boehm clarinet'. The mechanism remedies the sharp b natural, the flat f'' sharp and the very flat d''' sharp without new fingering, and is an invaluable addition to the accuracy of intonation.

The second development concerns the flute. Since the Boehm flute was designed in 1847, standard pitch has risen from something like a' 435 Hertz to a' 440 Hertz. To hold the instrument in tune with itself, the finger holes should, to keep pace with this development, have been placed closer to each other. This, however, did not happen; the change in pitch was accommodated entirely at the head end of the instrument rather than proportionally along its length. In other words, the instrument was being asked to perform at pitch a' 440 while continuing to be scaled as if the pitch were still a' 435 Hertz. Players and makers had become used to the instrument and its vagaries, and were happy to accept the instrument as they knew it. Albert Cooper, however, was not so disposed. In the 1950s he became convinced that the scaling of the flute was in need of correction. At that time he was working for Rudall Carte and Co, but by the late 1950s he had set up by himself, making instruments with a new, shorter, scaling. This became known as 'Cooper's scale', although it was, in fact, a scale more accurately tuned to equal temperament based on a' 440 Hertz. Although 'Cooper's scale' is not yet standard on all new flutes, many manufacturers in various parts of the world are now adopting it.

The final stage — tuning in performance
The technique of individual instruments is, at this, the final stage of tuning, of paramount importance. It is not simply a matter of knowing the general characteristics of a type of instrument, but also of coming to terms with the peculiarities of a particular

instrument. To arrive at some general principles, it is easier to start from particular cases than it is to generalise, in a vague way, about many different ones. Taking that much used (and much abused!) instrument the recorder, certain notes and types of fingering are always sources of trouble in intonation. Leaving aside the usual initial difficulties of making the lowest and highest notes on the instrument sound at all or without breaking at the wrong pitch, since these are matters of basic technique which most players overcome quite readily, the main sources of intonation difficulty are:

1 The hold for note g' on descant and tenor recorders (c'' on the treble and sopranino and c on the bass) fingered 1, 2, and 3 left hand with thumb hole closed.
2 The hold for e'' on descant and tenor (or a'' on treble and sopranino and a on bass) – the first standard pinched fingering.
3 All forked fingerings (ie those which have a gap in the fingering pattern).

The g' descant and similar fingerings on other instruments are flat and need to be blown up to be in tune with the rest of the instrument or with other, different, instruments. The note is immediately in conflict for volume and tone with its immediate neighbours f' sharp and g' sharp, which are both forked fingerings and therefore slightly sharp anyway, or not able to withstand any but the slightest breath pressure without going sharp in pitch and coarse in tone quality (the term 'wild' often being used to describe the effect). The standard fingering for the g' sharp usually produces a note which is too sharp in any case, and is much more likely to be in tune if fingered 1, 2, - 1, 2, 3 with thumb hole closed than it is with the orthodox 1, 2, - 1, 2, - fingering, but on some instruments the right-hand hole 3 should be either halved or shaded rather than fully closed.

The implications for technical difficulties are obvious; a note which, to be in tune, must be blown up, surrounded on each side by notes which cannot even readily take normal breath pressure without blowing wild, must be treated with respect. It must be practised often, with its immediate neighbours, to make the correct alterations to breath pressure for keeping the notes in tune, but at the same time the whole group of notes must be carefully judged so that the tone quality is not too markedly different.

The e'' descant fingering, and its corresponding notes on other instruments, is on the contrary sharp. It therefore blows wild very easily. This runs contrary to the general tendency on the instrument that the higher the note the more breath pressure it appears to need. This feeling can be misleading. The lowest notes on the instrument need very little breath pressure and some of the higher ones need a well-controlled draught of air at a greater pressure than for the low notes, but it is too much of a generalisation that the pressure must increase as the note rises in pitch. The feeling that it should is partially due to the excitement of the higher sound which can lead an inexperienced player to equate excitement with greater breath pressure. A general increase in breath pressure will inevitably lead to coarse tone and sharp intonation. Excitement can sometimes be conveyed by giving an 'edge' to the sound, which usually means making it slightly sharper and slightly coarser, but the decision to do so must be consciously made and its execution finely controlled if the borderline between artistry and vulgarity is not to be crossed.

Most forked fingerings are as similarly unstable as the descant e'' and its counterparts on other instruments. These notes should be played and listened to carefully so that the restrictions imposed on them by the acoustical properties of the instrument can be thoroughly understood. Since it is the perennial problem of intonation versus tone quality, final judgements about the fine placing of notes must be, as explained in Chapter 3, in relation to their melodic and harmonic functions.

These are some of the general characteristics of recorders, although the comments only begin to scratch the surface of discussion about intonation on recorders. Particular instances are also relevant. Taking three different qualities of recorder, the first a descant of good quality, made of African blackwood, the second a treble of fair quality made of rosewood and the third a plastic descant, the following characteristics become apparent. The good quality descant, although displaying the characteristics of sharpness and flatness described, has been skilfully tuned to bring the deficiences down to a minimum. The f' sharp and the g' sharp, although not so stable as the non-forked fingerings close to them, can be brought into tune with little variation in tone quality. The variation does exist, but there is sufficient latitude to allow for adequate matching. The treble presents different problems. Again the characteristic flat and sharp notes are present. On the treble they are c'' flat, a'' and forked fingerings sharp. Unfortunatley, the g'' is also slightly flat. This, being next to a sharp a'', means that care is needed, otherwise a strong g'' will be followed by a weak a'', or a flat g'' by a sharp a''. All playing round this area of the instrument has to be carefully matched. The plastic descant is a very different creature. Generally speaking, it is easier to keep in tune than the other two, but it is not so easy to match the tone quality. The characteristic flat and sharp notes are present, but the f' sharp, although reasonably well in tune, will only accept a certain breath pressure or it breaks to a slightly out of tune tenth above, and the e'' is similarly very unstable.

These specific instances show some of the principles involved in playing in tune after the designer and craftsmen have produced an instrument conforming to a certain specification. The same principles apply to all types of woodwind and brass instruments, and, simply stated, are:

1 Get to know the characteristics of the type of instrument you are playing – they can be found from a good technical instruction book or a teacher.
2 Get to know the individual characteristics of the instrument you are playing; listen carefully to it and where necessary take advantage of *all* the adjustments the manufacturer has provided.
3 Take note of the suggestions listed in Chapter 3 in connexion with intonation.

Woodwind instruments have less latitude in intonation than brass. The clarinet, for instance, is difficult to blow up in pitch, because an increase in pressure is more likely to stop the reed from vibrating than it is to increase the pitch; it can be 'farmed' down in pitch, but the latitude is not great. Adding a further category, strings, in which the instruments are infinitely variable in pitch without loss in quality, the woodwind players have the most difficult task of intonation. If either of the other groups move the pitch, even by a small amount (and the direction is usually upwards), the woodwinds are in trouble. In Chapter 1, Bottrigari's objections to various types of instrument playing together were quoted. They now, perhaps, begin to make more sense. Since 1594 advances have been made in the design and manufacture of instruments and the continuous use of vibrato has tended to blur the edges of intonation. Without these refinements we too might be joining Bottrigari in his condemnation of the practice of putting together different types of instrument to form an orchestra.

6
STRINGED INSTRUMENTS

From the point of view of tuning, stringed instruments appear to resolve themselves into two fundamentally different categories, roughly approximating to the instruments discussed at the beginning of Chapter 1; those which tune and those which temper. It is debatable, however, whether musicians strictly adhere to these general categories. In principle, they must, because an instrument can only be tuned in pure or tempered intervals, but in practice they need not, because where a number of intervals is concerned, some may be pure and others tempered.

The construction of the instrument should be some guide, unfretted instruments being likely to tune in pure and fretted instruments in tempered intervals, but this is by no means a sure way. Violinists, who would normally be expected to tune in pure intervals, have at times been advised to tune directly from the keyboard using tempered intervals, while performers on viols, which are fretted instruments and might therefore be expected to temper, tend to tune and to play in pure intervals.

As with other aspects of tuning, stringed instruments defy easy and rigid classification. But this is as it should be. Instruments have evolved to make music, not to satisfy the collecting, classifying and codifying desires of theorists and academics. To be a vital and continuously contemporary means of expression and communication, music must be allowed to evolve freely and not be constricted by codification and classification. Nevertheless, it is only possible to look at the past and the present.

In a guide, it is not possible to cover the historic tunings of every instrument, but it would be a poor guide that did not point out that a great variety of tuning has existed and still exists. Books on specific instruments, and the larger musical dictionaries, give details of many historic tunings, but modern instruments are designed for modern tunings, and many old instruments have been adapted to accept them also. A word of warning; when deviating from standard tunings, take care to see that the strings and the instrument itself have the tolerance to accept any new stresses and strains which might be imposed on them. This should not deter the seeker after truth. Historical accuracy can be a fickle companion, constantly changing as more and more research reveals the wealth of means by which musicians have sought to express themselves, but, paradoxically, it can also be a constant companion. History is always with us, despite Henry Ford's opinion of it, and it can still offer ways of looking and listening which it would be foolish to ignore.

Truth is not the prerogative of today, but it makes sense for a guide to begin by looking at what exists. Before considering the particular, some factors are common to all stringed instruments.

Unlike a keyboard instrument, there is no scale, as such, to set on a stringed instrument. If an instrument has frets, a scale will automatically be formed by tuning the individual strings, but in such cases it is built into the instrument, and it is not in the hands of the performer to make drastic alterations to it. This is not so with fretted instruments made in the traditional fashion by having pieces of gut tied round the finger-board to form the frets, and tied with a special type of knot. With these instruments the performer has the opportunity to alter the position of the frets, and therefore alter the scale, with the attendant responsibility of devising and setting another. With unfretted instruments, the performer selects the scale by stopping the string without the aid (or hindrance) of frets. As explained in Chapter 3 (page 54), there is no obligation on the part of the performer to include in a scale any but the lowest open string, and even this need only be included if appropriate.

Like keyboard instruments, stringed instruments are tuned by interval. Although they vary with the type of instrument, the intervals used are similar in both cases, mainly fifths or fourths, with the addition of a major third and an octave on some instruments. Other intervals are not generally favoured for tuning purposes.

There are fewer strings to tune, and consequently fewer intervals to set, on a stringed instrument than on a keyboard instrument. There must always be one less interval than the number of strings, since, by definition, an interval is the distance between two notes. The only deviation from this is for an instrument which has more than one string at a particular pitch, but even then, a unison is an interval which needs to be tuned.

Stringed instrument players do their own tuning. It would be most unusual to hear of a violinist calling in a professional tuner! Consequently there are almost as many ways of tuning as there are players.

Stringed instrument players do not usually count beats when tuning. Firstly, because the strings are fewer in number, a slight discrepancy would not be compounded in the same way as it could on a keyboard, and secondly, because any slight discrepancy could easily be adjusted in making the notes on the finger-board during performance. Thirdly, and perhaps more importantly, when an interval is pure, the tone on a stringed instrument seems to reflect that purity. Although the quality of tone must, to some extent, be affected by beating, it is the general effect of tone quality rather than beats or the lack of them which is most obvious.

Because a stringed instrument player does not set out deliberately to count beats, a slow beat could creep into the tuning by accident rather than design. On a keyboard, even a small amount of beating on a fifth could alter the temperament completely. Since the size of the fifth does not necessarily determine the size of the major third on a stringed instrument, a slow beat would cause no trouble.

The genus 'stringed instrument' includes many species. It includes both stable alterable and entirely alterable instruments as well as distinct families within even these subdivisions. These factors too have some influence on tuning, as does the fact that some of the instruments are usually bowed but can be plucked, while others are plucked in various ways, but are never bowed.

Irregular tunings are a feature of stringed instruments. At present, one type of tuning dominates keyboard instruments, but while there are standard tunings on strings, non-standard tunings are also expected; so much so that there is a term, *scordatura*, which means abnormal tuning. It is used in many types of music to help difficult passages, to obtain unusual chords, and to alter the tone colour.

Fretted and non-fretted instruments

The purpose of a fret is to make the sound of each string on an instrument, 'open'. The difference between stopped and open strings can be demonstrated on a violin. Play a sustained note on any open string, then press down the same string with the index finger about 1in from the nut, and again play a sustained note. Two things will be immediately obvious: a rise in pitch and an alteration in tone quality. Both are caused by the shortening of the string. The rise in pitch is due solely to the shorter vibrating length of string and the alteration in tone quality is due to the method of shortening. Try the same experiment again, this time using a piece of old violin string placed across the finger-board, like a guitar fret, at about 1in from the nut. Stop the string by placing the finger between the nut and the home-made fret. The tone quality of the original open string and the new note being played will be similar, only the pitch will be different. The fret will have acted like another nut further along the string.

On a fretted instrument, with the note played from behind, not over, the fret, the tone quality will be that of an open string. If the finger is placed over, and not behind, the fret, the tone quality will depend on how much the softness of the finger mitigates the effect of the hard, sharp edge of the fret. The softer effect of a stopped string is caused by the speaking length being defined, less clearly, by a softer medium than the sharp edge of the nut or fret.

The violin family

The violin family, consisting of the violin, the viola, the violoncello and, with some reservations, the double bass, is the basis of the orchestra. The characteristic broad-shouldered, full-bellied shape is common to all the family and immediately distinguishes it from other types of families of stringed instrument. The instruments have four strings, except for some double basses which have five, and the interval between the strings is a fifth, except again for the double bass where it is a fourth with possibly a major third between the two lowest strings on a five-stringed instrument.

A detailed description of the instruments is unnecessary for tuning purposes, but certain relevant factors require consideration. Many of these are common to all members of the family, differing only in size for each instrument. As with all stringed instruments, the speaking length of an open string is defined by the nut at one end and the bridge at the other. The string is fixed at one end and at the other it is adjustable for tuning, but on instruments with steel strings, adjusters are fitted to the tailpiece end (which is usually firmly fixed), to allow for fine adjustments to the tuning.

At the fixed, or adjuster-controlled end, the string is fastened to the tailpiece. The tailpiece itself is fixed to the instrument by

Figure 3 **Details** of outer shape of violin

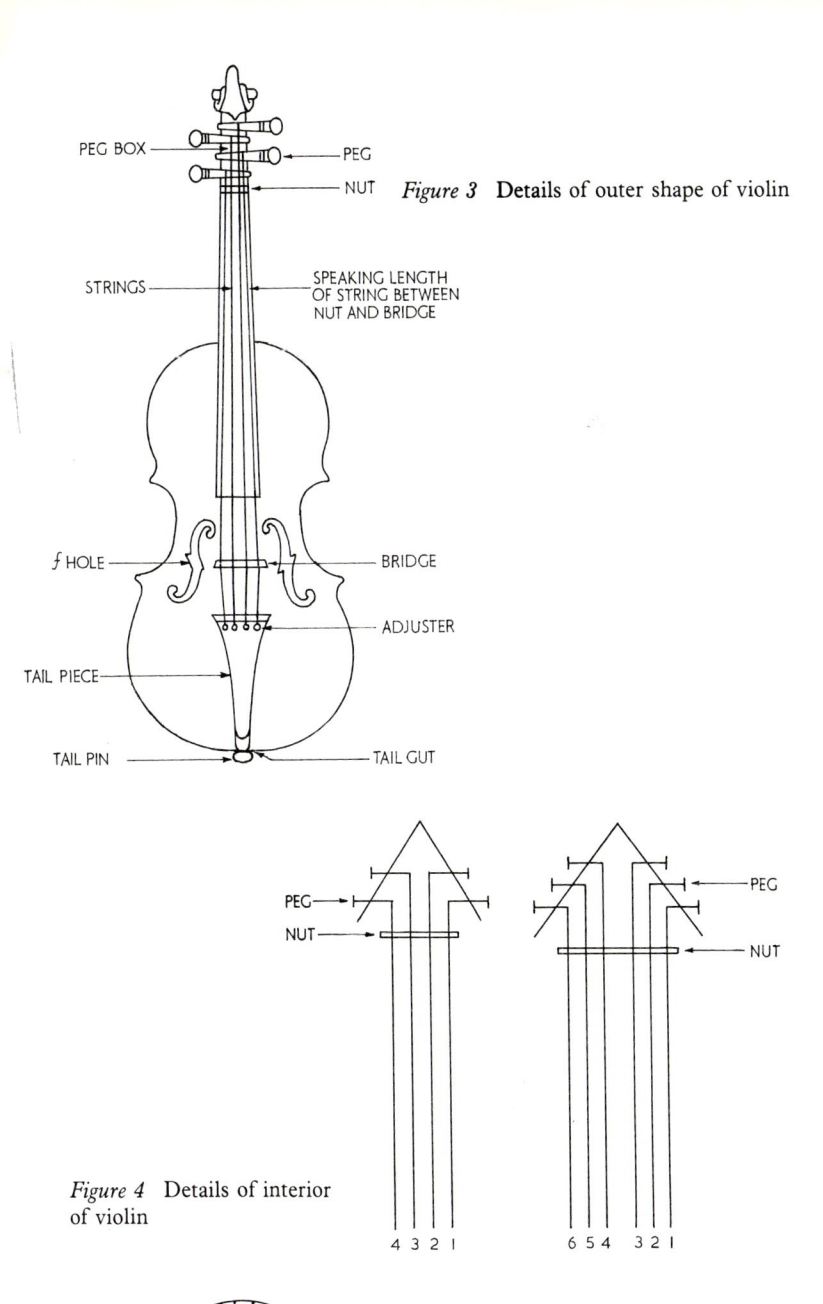

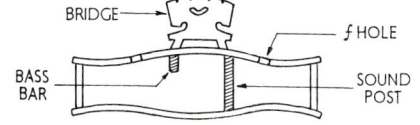

Figure 4 Details of interior of violin

Figure 5 Order of fixing strings

means of a tailgut, which in turn is fixed to the instrument by a tail pin embedded in the body of the instrument. Where adjusters are fitted, they are attached through the holes in the tailpiece; otherwise the strings themselves are fixed into these holes. The strings, coming from tailpiece or adjusters, pass over the bridge, then over the nut and are eventually fastened to tuning pegs which are slotted through holes in each side of the peg box. The pegs themselves are tapered to make a driving fit, which stops them from unwinding when the strings are at tension. The pegs on a double bass are of a different pattern. The strings are fitted to the pegs shown in the representational drawing at Figure 4. By thinking of the peg box as a V-shape, fitting strings to the correct peg is simplified.

The sound is transmitted from the strings to the main body of the instrument, which forms a resonating box, by the bridge. The bridge is assisted in this function by two components inside the instrument, the bass bar and the sound-post. Their position within the instrument is shown in Figure 5. These seemingly small elements are vital to the tone. Of the violin, Edward Heron-Allen, in his authoritative book *Violin making as it was and is*, has this to say:

> *The Sound Post*, with the *Bass Bar*, constitutes the entire nervous system of the fiddle, and on their proper construction and position depends the tone of the instrument. By a wrong arrangement of the sound post or bass bar, what are termed 'wolf notes' are produced, and when present, they may generally be cured by the proper adjustment of the bar or post. The sound post is a little round stick of fine, even-grained pine, varying, of course, in length with the distance from each other of the back and belly of the fiddle, both of which it must just firmly touch. It must not be long enough to force the back and belly apart ever so slightly, and must not be so short as to fall down when the instrument receives a jerk or when the strings are let down. . . . Its exact position depends entirely upon the quality and peculiarities of the fiddle, and must be carefully regulated by an experienced workman, but is almost invariably within ¼ inch behind the right foot of the bridge. . . .

The bass bar is a piece 'of fine soft, even-grained pine, about 10½ inches long which extends along the belly of the fiddle in a slightly oblique direction, underneath the left foot of the bridge' (the quotation is again from Héron-Allen).

The adjustments necessary for tuning are generally small, and the strings, bridge and pegs are quite vulnerable. The strings, of course, are particularly so. A single broken string can readily be replaced, provided there has been no damage done to the instrument. If the other strings are properly in place, it is a simple matter to copy the method used when fitting a new one. The new string must match the strings already on the instrument in quality or the tone will be uneven; but of course a new string will stretch, and consequently will go flat more readily than the others.

If all the strings are to be replaced, it is easier to remove one string at a time, replacing it with a new one as you go. This removes the necessity of replacing the bridge, and also means that the sound-post is less likely to fall.

The pegs, because of their taper, act like wedges when pressure is applied to them. They must fit firmly into the holes in the peg box, otherwise they may slip, but if they are pushed in too strongly, the pegs themselves may be damaged or the peg box could be split. Undue force, as in tuning a keyboard instrument, is to be avoided. Many a string has been broken by the application of too much force, but strings, although costly enough, can easily be replaced, whereas damage to the instrument could be much more troublesome. The double bass has a different type of peg from the other members of the family, details of which will be given later.

If the bridge is down, proceed, as you might do in other circumstances, with caution. Check first to see if it is damaged; if not it can be safely reset. Before setting up a fallen bridge, always check to see that the sound-post is in place. If not, it must be put back in its proper position before any pressure is put on the bridge. Should the instrument be set up and tuned with the sound-post down, the pressure could cause the belly of the instrument to split, or even to collapse completely. It may not always do so, but the risk is not worth taking.

Setting up a sound-post is a tricky operation. It is done by using a sound-post setter. This is a serpentine-shaped tool with a sharp point at one end and an array of cup-shaped openings at the other. The sharp point should be stuck into the sound-post (there will probably be a mark on the post to show where this has been done before) and the post made upright. The post should then be inserted through the right *f* hole, after making sure that the shaping on the top and bottom of the post will help to wedge it in position inside the instrument. The exact positioning of the sound-post is a matter of trial and error, but it will be close to, but behind, the right foot of the bridge. There will possibly be marks inside the instrument to show where the post has been, but if not, the position of the bridge can be assessed by taking an imaginary line across the belly of the instrument from the middle notch of one *f*-hole to the middle notch of the other. The feet of the bridge will be placed on this line, and the bridge itself will be midway between the two *f*-holes. Having established where the right foot of the bridge will be, the sound-post can be set.

When erecting the bridge, make sure that it is the right way round. The shaping across the top of the bridge is not uniform, but higher at one side than the other. The lower strings pass over the higher end of the bridge. Once the sound-post and bridge are in place (the strings should be made slack enough, when putting up the bridge, to allow it to be moved, but taut enough to hold it upright), the instrument can be tuned.

If the bridge has been damaged and needs to be replaced, do not get rid of the old bridge but use it as a pattern for shaping the new. Again the operation is tricky. The bridge must be shaped to fit the instrument. Begin with the feet. They should fit the belly of the instrument exactly and should be as thin as is practicable, not more than $\frac{1}{16}$in in the case of the violin and proportionate for the larger instruments. To assist in the final shaping, a piece of sandpaper can be placed face up across the belly of the instrument and the bridge rubbed along it so that the feet take on the exact arched shape of the belly. Having done this, the top should be shaped using the old bridge as a pattern. The curve of the bridge should be correct and its height must be such that the strings can be pressed to the finger-board without stress. The bridge should then be thinned down with a fine file or sandpaper so that the side of the bridge nearest the tailpiece remains perpendicular and the side nearest the finger-board is tapered, making the top of the bridge slightly thinner than the bottom. This again is a job requiring skill and experience and should not be undertaken lightly. The pattern of the damaged bridge is invaluable; without it, the amateur would be well advised to seek expert assistance.

Although the setting up procedures described are not generally part of the tuning process, the instrument cannot be tuned and played unless it is properly set up. As to the tuning itself, since there are only four strings, tuning is straightforward. An *a'* should be taken from a tuning fork, pitch pipe, piano or similar source and the *a'* string tuned as a perfect unison with it. The other three strings should then be tuned in pure fifths. It is possible to tune a violin by listening for beats. Starting from an a', play strings a' and e'' together and listen for the harmonic at pitch e'''. It should be clearly audible when both strings are bowed or plucked together, but, unlike a keyboard instrument, it is not always easy to hear the required harmonic when the string is played by itself. For this reason, it is much easier to learn to listen for harmonics from a piano note than it is from the same note played on a violin, although they are more readily audible on the lower strings, particularly on the violoncello. Listen to the harmonic at e''', and by adjusting the e'' string, remove all beats at this pitch; the fifth a' to e'' will then be pure. Starting again from a', play strings a' and d' together, listen for the harmonic at pitch a'', remove all beats at this pitch and the a' to d' fifth will then be pure. Finally starting from the d' string, play the d' and g strings together, listen for the harmonic at pitch d'', and by removing all beats at this pitch by adjusting the g string, the fifth d' to g will be pure. If the pitch has been taken from the piano, check the a' string with the piano again to see that it is still in tune; if so, check the g string with the piano g. There should be a slow beat (approximately half a metronome setting of 53), the violin being slightly flatter than the piano. This is because the fifths on the violin will be pure (702 cents) and the fifths on the piano are narrow (700 cents). Tuning down from a' to g means tuning two fifths; there will therefore be a discrepancy of 4 cents between the gs produced by each of the systems. When the notes are played consecutively there will be little or no difference between them, but if played together, they will produce the slow beat mentioned.

Most string players would not bother to count beats – they would play the adjacent strings together as suggested above, and then judge by the warmth of tone when the instrument was in tune. If there are discrepancies in the fifths when tuning, the tone sounds rather thinner and niggardly by comparison with pure fifths. This thinness of tone applies only to fifths and other intervals which should be pure, not to the instrument as a whole. A good player can play in tune and with beautiful tone even when the tuning notes on his instrument have slipped out of pitch.

There have been suggestions at various times that the fifths on a violin need not be pure. J. J. Quantz, in his book entitled *On Playing the Flute*, published in Berlin in 1752, wrote:

To tune the violin accurately, I think you will not do badly to follow the rule that must be observed in tuning the keyboard, namely, that the fifths must be tuned a little on the flat side rather than quite truly or a little sharp, as is usually the case, so that the open strings will all agree with the keyboard.

With equal temperament as standard, there is at least a modicum of sense in the argument that all instruments should conform to that system. In theory, at least, it appears to make playing together more likely to be in tune. But modicum is the correct word. Since only three intervals (four notes) are tuned on a violin and all the others 'made' by the player, and it is well known that string players tend to push up the pitch, add to this a touch of vibrato which will confuse the issue still futher, and the term equal temperament begins to have little or no meaning. Besides, equal temperament would be difficult to set accurately on a stringed instrument without frets. It could only be done in two ways. The first would be to count beats when tuning the fifths, as on a keyboard, and the second is to copy the pitch for each string from another source already tuned to equal temperament. Neither of these methods is wholly satisfactory. Counting beats would be a laborious business, and copying a note at the octave or unison from some other source, by ear, would not be accurate enough to be sure that, when each note had been copied, each fifth would be precisely two cents narrower than true. No string player aims to tune in either of these fashions; he just tunes 'in fifths' (or 'in fourths' for the double bass), and if the interval is a few cents, or beats, too wide or narrow, although it would affect the resonant feeling of the instrument during tuning, it would have very little bearing in the tuning of other notes.

The violin

Whatever its size, except for specialist violins like the *violino piccolo* required in Bach's Brandenburg Concerto No 1, the tuning notes are e'', a', d' and g, note a' being taken from another source to begin the tuning. Sizes of instrument vary. The most usual are full, three-quarter, half, quarter and one eighth. The smaller instruments are intended for young beginners; all players eventually graduate to a full-size instrument. The methods of setting up sound-posts and bridges have been described. Adjusters for fine tuning are fitted when steel strings are used, and could necessitate slight modifications to the tailpiece. If the holes on the tailpiece through which the strings are normally fixed will not allow the adjuster to seat firmly and comfortably, they may need to be enlarged with a countersink tool. It is also possible that when the adjuster is fitted, the end of the string is fouling the tailpiece. If this happens, a shaving should be taken off the tailpiece to allow clearance.

The smaller the violin, the more critical the tuning process becomes. A slight increase or decrease in tension on the strings of a small violin will cause a greater alteration in pitch than it will on a larger instrument. Guard against broken strings; make each movement of the peg small.

The viola
Except for the tuning notes, which are a', d', g and c, the a' still being the note taken from another source, comment on setting up and tuning is much the same as for other stringed instruments, particularly the violin. The viola, being a larger instrument than the violin, does however have its own strings, bows etc, and it is inadvisable to use violin parts except in an emergency, in which case the resultant alteration in sound will have to be endured until the correct parts are available. A violin sound-post setter is suitable for a viola, and the suggestions on fitting adjusters are as for the violin. For young players, a violin can be strung as a viola, with the resultant lack of tone quality, until it is possible to manage a full-size instrument.

The violoncello
The general information on strings is appropriate for the cello too, but the question of size needs to be considered. The feet of the bridge, for instance, although still as fine as practicable, will be thicker than for the violin, and the sound-post setter is much larger. The height of the strings above the finger-board at its bridge end is also greater than for the violin, but this is not relative to the sizes of the instruments. There will not be a lot of difference in the string height. Since this is determined by the bridge, it is seldom a thing which the amateur needs to set, and as with other stringed instruments the complete shaping of a bridge is best left to someone with experience, or attempted only under supervision. The tuning notes are an octave lower than those of the viola, namely, a, d, G and C. The tuning is again done from an A, not infrequently from the same a' as the violin and viola.

The double bass

Many of the preceding comments have been qualified by the words 'except for the double bass'. The reasons for this lie in the ancestry of the instrument. Although it is used as the bass of the violin family, it is more correctly the bass of the viol family. Most basses have the characteristic sloping shoulders of the viol family, and even those which have the squared shoulders of the violin family are not treated like other members of that family either in tuning interval or, quite frequently, in bowing technique. Apart from size, there are other differences too. The pegs are not of the simple taper type like the other members of the violin family, but are of the worm and cog type, and are often known as machine pegs rather than just pegs. There are various qualities of machine peg depending on the quality and price of the instrument, but they are usually of the half-plate (two pegs fitted on one brass plate) or the quarter-plate (each peg fitted to a separate brass plate) type.

The tuning interval is different too; the double bass is tuned in fourths like the viols, unlike the violins which are tuned in fifths. The written tuning notes are *g*, *d*, A and E, but they sound an octave lower than the written pitch. Because the pitch of the instrument is so low, the definition of its notes is less clear. Harmonics are audible, particularly from the three upper strings, but should be treated with care, because they may not always be accurate. If they are used, they should first be checked for pitch and then, when tuning, the fourth harmonic of the lower note should be in unison with the third harmonic of the upper, as described in Chapter 2, page 26. The two upper strings are easier to hear in tune than the lower two. Practice and careful listening are needed to learn about each individual instrument. Listen to each string and check the harmonics it gives; use a piano to help as suggested on page 24; only then will it be safe to use them.

Some double basses have a fifth string tuned to low C, to make the lowest note exactly an octave below the cello. Others have an attachment, invented by Poike Glaesels, fitted to the scroll which extends the length of the E string on a four string bass, to low C or B. It is played by keys fitted to the attachment.

The rebec

This is often considered to be one of the ancestors of the violin. It is a bowed instrument. It has neither frets nor sound-post. The instrument most used today is the soprano, tuned *a'*, *d'*, *g*.

Fretted instruments

This group of instruments includes the viols, the guitar, the lute, the ukulele, the mandolin and, usually, the banjo. Some brief comment has already been made about frets, but it is easier to describe their function in connection with a particular instrument. To save repetition, this has been done when describing the members of the viol family, and only specific details worthy of notice, such as tuning notes, have been given for the other fretted instruments.

The viols

Most descriptions of the members of the viol family refer at first to the general shape of the instrument, particularly its sloping shoulders and fatter body shape, when compared with the violin family. Gerald R. Hayes, in the second volume of *Musical Instruments and their Music*, entitled 'The Viol, and other bowed instruments', prefers the following:

> Those elements that combine together to make a viol must be considered in two respects, the one absolute and the other, for present convenience, in relation to the violins.
>
> Those absolute are:
> 1. The number of strings
> 2. The tuning of the strings
> 3. The gut frets upon the finger board
> 4. The manner of bowing
> and, relative to the family of the violins,
> 5. The strings are lighter, longer, and less tense
> 6. The wood is much thinner throughout
> 7. The ribs, especially in the smaller instruments, are usually deeper.
>
> No mention is made here of those features of bodily shape that have so often been given for the identification of a viol.

The standard number of strings is six (although there have been references to five-, four- and even three-stringed viols). The strings are usually tuned in perfect fourths with the addition of a major third, the instruments are fretted and they are all held downward when played.

One of the fundamental differences between viols and violins is the use of frets. They have two functions; to show the positions of the semitones on each string, and to make each string act always as an open string. Reference has already been made to the differences in sound between a stopped and an open string, but it is the question of semitonal divisions by using frets which is most vexed. It can be argued that there is little point in having frets if they do not show where the semitones are, and if they do show them, correctly for each string, they must, of necessity, make the instrument equally tempered. Using Bottrigari as an authority again, in *Il Desiderio* he states: 'The Lute and Viol sound two equal semitones, that is a tone divided into two equal semitones according to the idea of Aristoxenus.' (By dividing the tetrachord or the notes forming a perfect fourth, into thirty equal parts and giving twelve parts to each tone and six to each semitone, in his syntonic diatonic, it is often considered that Aristoxenus was describing equal temperament, but opinions are divided on this.) The idea of equality in temperament still persists in modern writing when frets are discussed. Gerald R. Hayes writes:

> Musically, the purpose of frets is twofold: they give to each note played the clear ringing quality of the open string, so characteristic of the instruments [the viol]; and they provide for an equally tempered scale.

Although stating that the frets 'provide for an equally tempered scale' (a skilful method of not confirming that they actually form one), the writer later adds: 'The purist in solo playing is not hindered by the frets from obtaining his perfect consonances.' This appears to introduce a new type of conflict, that between player and instrument. An instrument designed to play in equal temperament lacks perfect consonances, except for octaves. The player could also be in conflict with the instrument in tuning. If the frets imply equal temperament and the instrument is tuned in fourths with the addition of one major third, these intervals would have to be tempered (by two and fourteen cents too wide, respectively); if not, the method of tuning will not meet the intention of the frets. But viol players do play in consonant intervals. Like the holds on wind instruments, the frets indicate the approximate position of the note, but it is up to the player to convert that approximation into an exact position to suit the occasion. It is not true to say that because the instrument has frets it is much easier to play it in tune than it is to play a stringed instrument without frets. The player must bring the note to an appropriate pitch by playing behind the frets, over the frets, or by pulling or pushing the string; accepting the position of the note as the fret suggests, is not sufficient.

The tuning of viols

A consort of viols consists of treble, alto (or more correctly, perhaps, counter-tenor), tenor and bass instruments. The latter is more commonly known as the viola da gamba, or 'leg' viol, although all members are played in 'leg' rather than 'arm' fashion. There is also a *pardessus de viole* which is smaller and of a higher pitch than the treble. It is a solo rather than a consort instrument and often has only five strings; the lowest string, shown in brackets in the table which follows, would in this case be the string which was omitted. The other instruments all have six strings.

Probably the most quoted method of tuning the viol is that given by John Playford in *An Introduction to the Skill of Musick*. The following is taken from page 93 of the 1674 edition. After stating that there are two methods, 'one by Tablature or Letters, the other by the Gam – ut Rule', of the letters he says: 'The letters are Eight, A, B, C, D, E, F, G, H, seven of these are assigned to the seven frets on the Neck of the Viol, A is for the string open, so B is the first fret, C, the second, D, the third, E, the fourth, F, the fifth, G, the sixth and H, the seventh.' He then goes on to describe the actual method of tuning:

> When you begin to Tune, raise your Treble or smallest string as high as conveniently it will bear without breaking; then stop only your second or Small Mean in F, and tune it till it agree in sound with your Treble open; that done, stop your Third in F, and make it agree with your Second open; then stop your Fourth in F, and make it agree with your Third open; then stop your Fifth in F, and make it agree with your Fourth open; and lastly, stop your Sixth in F, and make it agree to your Fifth open. This being exactly done, you will find your Viol in Tune.

Although the actual pitch of the instrument would be, to say the least, arbitrary, since the direction 'raise your Treble or smallest string as high as conveniently it will bear' is hardly a clear indication of pitch, this method would, if the frets were set to give equal semitones, produce an equally tempered scale. If they were set by the 'rule of the eighteenth', each semitone would be 99 cents, just short of the 100 cents required for equal temperament.

The second method suggested by Playford is that of naming the actual note to which each string should be tuned, and is the more reliable for pitch. The notes in general use today for each instrument are given below. The numbers are for the strings, highest to lowest, not, as in Playford, the frets also:

	1	2	3	4	5	6	
The Pardessus	g''	d''	a'	e'	c'	(g)	
The Treble	d''	a'	e'	c'	g	d	
The Alto (Counter-tenor)	c''	g'	d'	a'	f	c	
The Tenor	g'	d'	a	f	c	G	
The Bass	d'	a	e	c	G	D	(A)

Alternatives to these are required for certain compositions.

At first, the strings are tuned in fourths and thirds, but having reached the bottom string, final checks and adjustments are then made. The outer strings must be exactly at the double octave, and on those instruments which have the major third between string 3 and 4, the interval between strings 1 and 5 will be a twelfth (or compound fifth) and so will the interval between strings 2 and 6. These two compound fifths should be tuned true. The major third between strings 3 and 4 will finally be set by checking in octaves. Taking the bass viol as the example, the g on the e string (string 3) will be checked as a pure octave with the open G string (string 5), and the g on the c string (string 4) must be in unison with the g on the e string (string 3). Had all the fourths been tuned pure (498 cents) and the double octave d' – D been pure (2400 cents), the major third c – e must be a full comma too wide. By tuning in the way described, the major third turns out to be equally tempered (400 cents), and the G – c and e – a fourths are slightly wide. The comma is therefore distributed over a wider area and not confined to the major third. An irregular temperament is formed by tuning in this fashion, which will necessitate pitch alterations at various times to allow for playing in consonant intervals as far as possible. The figures quoted are of course approximate, since players may not, by listening intently to remove all beating however slow, stick exactly to acoustically pure intervals. Nor need they; a slow beat would affect the playing little, if at all. The important fact to emerge is that the tempering of the instrument cannot be equal, even if one of the intervals happens to be so, if it is arrived at by accepting pure octaves and some pure fifths as fine tuning checks. The other viols would, of course, be tuned and checked in a similar manner although the pitches of the notes would be different.

On viols, the true intonation is not blurred by vibrato. Nathalie Dolmetsch points out in Lesson 1 of *Twelve Lessons on the Viola da Gamba* that Marin Marais, the great French composer for and virtuoso on the viol, 'has an elaborate system of signs, including two for different types of *vibrato*. This is used most sparingly, on the important notes only, in expressive pieces. Thus used it tells amazingly and moves the hearer far more than on the violin, where it is never wholly absent. In lively gay music it is not used at all; it is not needed.'

Setting up is similar to other stringed instruments. The changing of strings, erection of bridges and sound-post, and the shaping of bridges are all done in a similar fashion. Bridges are much less arched than those of the violin family and care must be taken because the wood used in the construction of a viol is very thin. Apart from the changing of strings, which is a simple operation, the other aspects of setting up should be treated with caution. A poorly set up instrument will never respond well, and expert advice should always be sought in cases of doubt.

Playing in consort

As with brass and woodwind instruments, the fine adjustments to the tuning which a performer makes come more into the realm of instrumental technique than they do into general discussion of tuning, but again, some general points do emerge. Playing over the frets as well as behind them has already been discussed, but pushing and pulling the strings have only been given, so far, a passing mention. They are used as a final resort when other methods of keeping truly in tune are not effective. In pushing the string, the pressure a player applies to the fret is directed toward the bridge. This has the effect of slackening the speaking length of the string slightly, and therefore lowering the pitch. conversely, in pulling the string, the performer applies pressure away from the bridge, in the direction of the nut. This tightens the speaking length of the string, thus sharpening the note.

These devices, as well as careful listening to intervals when tuning, may well keep an instrument in tune with itself, but because the tuning system produces an irregular temperament, the instruments, in consort, may not agree with each other. Viol players, therefore, need a period of time in tuning to bring their instruments into accord with each other. After individual checking, they will play a few chords together to help iron out any discrepancies in the tunings.

The guitar

The guitar presents much the same problems of intonation as does the viol. The frets suggest equal temperament, but the performer, by playing over them where necessary, and by pushing and pulling the strings to produce the required nuances of intonation, plays in just intonation. The method of tuning, however, is not identical. Firstly, of course, the strings are tuned to different notes. The written pitches to which a guitar is tuned are e'', b', g', d', a and e, but they sound an octave lower.

Being a plucked instrument, the guitar is rich in harmonics and its resonance is such that many of these harmonics are reinforced and prolonged. Consequently, tuning by listening for beats is aurally tiring. A much better method would be to tune by using harmonics. Since they are pure sounds, harmonics are not obscured, a player selects those he requires and they are the only notes produced. By the elimination of all unnecessary sounds the accuracy of tuning should be enhanced. Unfortunately this is not always so, because strings are seldom consistent enough within themselves to produce acoustically correct harmonics, and so the system is not as safe and accurate as it should be.

By playing in just intonation, the instrument, like the viols, is set to an irregular temperament. It is necessary therefore to adjust it, depending on the key in which the music is to be played. These adjustments may be slight, but they are essential to accuracy in intonation. As a check, the performer will try over the main chords of the key in which the music is written, in much the same way as viol players in consort check the unanimity of their tuning, to see that they are correct. Although the tuning notes, frets, and, when they are correct, the harmonics, are guides, it is in the end the ear and judgement of the perfomer which counts in making fine adjustments to the set tuning and to the selection of each note and chord during performance.

The beginner on the guitar is not immediately confronted by these niceties. The usual method for such players is to tune from the bottom up. Tune the low e (sixth string) from a piano or pitch pipe (or some similar source), then, using the note produced by the fifth fret on that string, tune the a (fifth string) in unison with it. Starting now from the fifth string, by using the note produced by its fifth fret, tune the d' (fourth) string in unison with it. Similarly, from the fifth fret of the fourth (d') string, the g' (third) string is tuned as a unison. Since the second string is b', only a major third above g', the fourth fret of the g' string is used to tune the b' string as a unison. Finally the e'' (first) string is tuned as a double octave above the original e (sixth) string and checked against the note produced by the fifth fret of the second (b') string as a unison. This is very much the same method as that which John Playford recommended in 1674.

If a modern instrument has been accurately tuned using the frets only as guides, it should then be set to equal temperament. The method which has been most prevalent in the setting of frets since its use by Vincenzo Galilei (1581) is known as the 'rule of the eighteenth'. Galilei discovered that by setting each fret in the ration of 17:18, he got nearer to an equal tuning for each string than by setting them in any other method. He did not show any mathematical reasons for his choice, but by using the formula explained on page 40, it can be seen that this ratio gives the following cent value for a semitone:

Ratio 17:18 = 1:1.0588235
$\log_{10} 1.0588235 = .024823$
Using the multiplying factor 3986.3136
cent value = $.024823 \times 3986.3136$
= 98.954654

which, for all practical purposes gives a semitone of 99 cents.

This is very close to an equally tempered semitone of 100 cents, and modern makers have adjusted the 'rule of eighteenth' enough to produce true equally tempered semitones.

The lute

During its long and noble history, the lute has had many different tuning systems. Being a fretted instrument, it has the same sort of intonation difficulties and solutions as viols and the guitar. The most used methods of tuning are g', d', a, f, c, G or a', e', b, g, d, A, but round about 1640 the lutenist and composer Denis Gaultier introduced another system, f', d', a, f, d, A, called the *nouveau ton*, which continued to be used as long as the lute retained its popularity. However, the most usual tuning is g', d', a, f, c, G, the instrument having one string for its top note and two, tuned in unison, for every other tuning note. This disposition, with the addition of a further pair of strings taking the pitch down to D, was the instrument of John Dowland and other Elizabethan players and composers.

The mandolin(e)
This is also a member of the lute family, and has four or five courses of strings — a course being a pair of strings tuned in unison. The Neapolitan instrument is tuned as the violin to e'', a', d' and g, and the Milanese to e'', d'', a', c' and g. The instrument is played with a plectrum, by a continuous tremolo action.

The ukelele
This is a small guitar like instrument of Hawaiian origin. The usual tuning is a', d', f' sharp and b'.

The banjo
This is a stringed instrument, often fretted, with a long neck and a single-headed drum-like body made from parchment held taut by a hoop. It can have from five to nine strings. The most usual arrangement is five strings tuned g', c, g, b, d'. The highest string, known as the thumb string, is placed beside the lowest. The tuning peg for the thumb string is often situated half way down the finger-board rather than in the head of the instrument.

7
PERCUSSION INSTRUMENTS

Although there are many percussion instruments which give a note of definite pitch, few are actually tuned by the performer. It is the timpani, or kettle drums, which demand the greatest attention from a tuning guide. These instruments have a membrane (animal or man-made) stretched over the top of a bowl-shaped body usually of copper or fibre glass. The instruments come in various sizes and are tunable either by means of hand screws or by a pedal mechanism. Each instrument is usually variable in pitch by the maximum of a perfect fifth, but of course can only produce one note at a time, even though the pedal mechanism makes rapid tuning and *glissando* effects possible.

The pitch is altered by increasing and decreasing the tension of the membrane, and the pitch is produced because of the elasticity of that membrane. It must, therefore, be carefully treated. Never leave a drum with its membrane tightly stretched. When the instrument is not in use, the head should be slackened. String players take similar precautions with their bows. Unless the pressure is released when a bow is not in use, the stick can soon become distorted.

Timpani are normally used in groups of two or three. Authorities differ slightly on the pitch of these. The lowest drum can be set within the range E flat – B flat, or F – *c*, the middle pitched drum approximately in the range G – *d*, and the highest B flat – *f*, or *c* – *g*. It is much better for tone quality if the drums are not used at their extremes of pitch, although this is not always possible.

The acoustical properties of timpani are very complex. The fundamental note produced by the head dies away very quickly and is difficult to generate; it is therefore of little practical use. The other harmonics are not so readily damped. Because the fundamental is not of practical use, it is the second harmonic (the octave above the fundamental) which is accepted as the true pitch of the drum. The higher harmonics are not always in exact whole-number proportions to this harmonic and are consequently out of tune with it, giving rise to the somewhat indefinite pitch which is characteristic of timpani. This applies to a head uniformly stretched; if the streching was not uniform, the frequency of the harmonics could well be altered. Some harmonics, however, can be clearly heard and used in tuning. The third harmonic, a perfect fifth above the accepted pitch note is useful, as it is in the tuning of many other instruments.

In tuning timpani, the first difficulty to overcome is hearing the exact pitch of the note produced. This should, in theory, be easy, but because the drum is rich in harmonics, some of which may well not agree with the accepted pitch, careful listening to understand exactly what the instrument is saying, is essential. Things are further complicated because all the harmonics come into operation immediately the drum is struck, and this tends to give a boost to the original striking. Added to this, the actual striking of the drum head alters its tension, and, momentarily, its pitch. In listening for a drum note, it is best to ignore the initial strike note at first because of the complication attendant upon it, and concentrate instead on the continuous hum note which follows.

Taking the use of the word hum one step further in the discussion, James Blades, in his book, *Percussion Instruments and their History* states that a method which percussionists often use is to hum the note to which the drum is to be tuned with their lips close to the playing spot (that is the spot on the drum head which gives the best quality of sound), and when the drum responds with a singing tone, it is well in tune. To do this the drum head needs to be inclined and the players lips are very near to the drum skin, and gives rise to the suggestion that he is kissing it or whispering to it. The latter suggestion is nearer the truth − he is indeed whispering the correct note to it.

Drums often need to be tuned a fifth apart. This can readily be done by using the harmonic audible at a fifth above the accepted tuning note. To use this method, tune the lower of the two drums from some external source. When this is done, strike the tuned drum, and while altering the tension of the drum to be tuned, listen carefully until it begins to sing in unison with the audible harmonic at a fifth above the note of the tuned drum. When the drum being tuned begins to sing this note, it is accurately tuned. By using this method of sympathetic vibration, the drum being tuned need not be struck, and a pure fifth can be more accurately set. It would be possible to use other harmonics in this way if they were strong enough to make the second drum resonate in sympathy, but because of the inharmonic nature of many of them, they could be treacherous guides.

When tuning keyboard instruments, advice was given against holding a note in, or out of, tune with the tuning key, and the necessity of setting the pin to keep the string in tune was also stressed. Similar warnings are necessary with percussion instruments even though there are no pins to set. When a drum head has been tightened or slackened, it must be checked to make sure that it is not being held by the rim, otherwise the tension will alter after the first real strike. The position is very similar to equalising tension throughout a string. Pressure should be exerted on the drum head to help to equalise the tension, and this can be done by gently, but firmly, pressing on the drum head. On drums which are tuned by hand screws, a check should be made by tapping gently between the screws to make sure that tension is equal throughout the head.

Just as in other aspects of tuning, the fine tuning of percussion instruments depends on the aural ability of the player. Such ability can be developed by careful listening as explained in Chapters 1 to 3, but must be adapted to the special requirements of the instruments being tuned. It is all too easy to dismiss percussion instruments as being easy to tune, but, in fact, because of the richness and variety of their harmonics and the continuity of their resonance, they are simultaneously very difficult but very rewarding to study.

It is inadvisable to tamper with the tuning of xylophones, bells, glockenspiels and other forms of tuned percussion instruments. They are tuned before they leave the manufacturer, and though they can be altered, such alteration should not be attempted without specialised knowledge.

8
A GUIDE TO THE HISTORY OF TEMPERAMENT

Although in practice all music needs to be tempered, the term temperament is more closely associated with keyboards than with most other instruments. It is on a keyboard that the effects of temperament, or the lack of it, are most readily noticed. Other instruments may be designed to conform to equal temperament but it is only on a keyboard, and on the harp, that there can be no redemption from the sin of rigidity. Once the instrument has been tuned, it must stay that way; the player cannot alter its intonation. It is for this reason that discussion on, and experiments in, temperament have centred round these instruments, and to a lesser extent fretted instruments, more than any other. With the acceptance of equal temperament as standard, discussion of temperaments would appear to be only of academic or historical, rather than practical, interest. Such a view would have been more justified at the end of the nineteenth century than it is now. The final victory for equal temperament seemed then to have been won, after a long and hard rearguard action fought particularly by organists, and only a few pockets of resistance remained into the twentieth century. But mercifully the victory was not absolute, and we are now enjoying a revival of interest in sounds which had been thought by many to be extinct.

The revival came about because of the renewed interest in music and instruments of earlier times. To play early music in a temperament which is completely foreign to it is as unfeeling as trying to play Chopin on a virginals. A harpsichord, virginals, spinet or clavichord needs frequent tuning and many owners have quickly learned that the advantages of being able to tune their own instruments are not only financial. By turning what could be a chore and a nuisance into positive musical advantage, they are discovering the delights of using various temperaments more appropriate than equal for the music they wish to play. It is

A GUIDE TO THE HISTORY OF TEMPERAMENT 133

to be hoped that many others will join them as the knowledge of how to tune to these temperaments is more widely spread. This guide is intended as a help in choosing an appropriate temperament, rather than an historical resumé of methods of tempering. The appendix which follows gives detailed instructions on how to set some temperaments; more general information on how to work out a scheme for setting temperaments has already been given.

Temperaments fall into four main categories: Pythagorean, meantone, irregular and equal. All of these, in some shape or form, have been important, and historically they appeared in roughly the order in which they are given above.

About Pythagorean tuning little needs to be said. In its pure form it is not a practical proposition on a keyboard. By tuning in pure fifths, the major thirds are too wide for constant harmonic use, and the impossibility of combining pure fifths and pure octaves rule it out as even a possible starter on a keyboard. Modifications have been suggested and used, but many come more correctly into the category of irregular temperaments.

The various meantone temperaments are of much greater use than pure Pythagorean. The temperaments themselves are easy to describe, as well as being amenable to work out in figures, but in the writings of musicians and theorists it is not always clear exactly what form of meantone is intended. The most usual way of describing meantone temperaments is by reference to the division of the syntonic comma: ¼-comma, ⅕-comma, ²/₇-comma and the like. This description means that the usable fifths are made narrow by that proportion of the syntonic comma. In ⅕-comma meantone, for instance, the fifths are made narrow by one fifth of 22 cents, and therefore stand at 702 minus 4.4 cents, or 697.6 cents. The narrowing applies to all but one of the cycle of twelve fifths used in tuning.

Evidence of the use of meantone temperaments exists from at least 1482, in the writings of Bartolomeo Ramos de Pareia, and as late as 1812, in *An Essay on Perfect Intonation* by Henry Liston. The latter gives a table of five temperaments, about which he writes:

> The first of these systems of temperament, in which the Vth is diminished ¼ comma, is called the system of mean tones; the tempered tone being the mean betwixt the major and the minor tones, of the true diatonic scale. It is also called the vulgar temperament,

although the next scheme in which the Vth is diminished ⅕ comma, is more nearly what is in common use, it being the object not to tune the IIIds perfect but as much too sharp as the Vths are too flat. The third scheme, in which the fifth is flattened ⅙ comma, is that proposed by Mr. Hawkes. . . . The fourth scheme, in which the fifth is flattened ⁵⁄₁₈ comma, is that proposed by Dr. Smith, which he calls the system of equal harmony. . . . The last of these five schemes has been proposed by some in order to adapt the scale to the number of finger keys, as it nearly divides the scale into twelve equal semitones.

If we were to take these dates literally, as extremes, they include all the music of Bach, Handel, Mozart and Haydn, as well as all the Beethoven piano sonatas as far as Op 81a. Any of the meantone temperaments mentioned by Liston would create havoc with the harmonies of all the composers listed above, and Liston does not approve of the final system he mentions in the above extract, because the thirds and the sixths 'will be in every case, extremely disagreeable'. We, no doubt, would think differently. But Liston's comments cannot be dismissed as the views of an outmoded, conservative musical theorist, seeking statistical evidence to keep alive traditions in which he believes and which he sees being swept away. William Crotch, writing in the same year as Liston (*Elements of Composition*, 1812), makes the following references to temperament:

> As organs are at present tuned (with unequal temperament), keys which have many flats or sharps will not have a good effect, especially if the time be slow.

Later in the book he goes on to say, when referring to unequal temperament:

> Of this there are many systems which the student is now capable of examining himself. He will also find much amusement in studying the various attempts to improve the scale by increasing the number of notes in the octave.

He goes on to cite some instances of instruments which have such extra notes. In the second edition of the same work, in 1833, Crotch adds the following passage:

> The author, in conclusion, cannot but regret that the preference of English organists for the old method of tuning is (as he is informed) hitherto so strong and determined, as to have resisted and repelled the attempts made to introduce the equal temperament into our Cathedrals and Churches . . . he feels convinced that its practicability

and superiority are as unequivocal on the organ as they are allowed to be on the pianoforte ... in so doing, he is contending for the far higher authority of the judgement and practise of one whom, he trusts, his opponents must venerate and admire – the greatest of all composers for this sacred instrument – Sebastian Bach.

Even though Crotch is suggesting that pianos were generally tuned to equal temperament, the piano makers, John Broadwood & Son, did not accept it as standard for their instruments until 1846, even though Muzio Clementi in his *Introduction to the Art of Playing on the Piano Forte*, published in London in 1801, had written:

> Now, the inconvenience of charging the memory with the VARIOUS uses of the SAME keys, is but small; when compared with the impracticableness of performing on an instrument, furnished with keys, PERFECTLY corresponding with every flat, and sharp, single or double, which composition may require: a method therefore has been adopted in tuning, called TEMPERAMENT, which, by a small deviation from the truth of every interval, EXCEPT THE OCTAVE, renders the instrument capable of satisfying the ear in EVERY KEY.

Although he uses the word 'temperament' only, this statement applies more nearly to equal than to any other temperament. In 1879, Edgar Brinsmead, in his *History of the Pianoforte*, accepts equal temperament in the following terms:

> As the pianoforte is an imperfect instrument. . . . Hence the necessity of *tempering* the fourths and fifths which has given the new scale the name of equal temperament.

Clementi had accepted equal temperament for pianos in 1801, yet seventy-eight years later an English piano maker could still refer to it as 'new'. It is significant, too, of the attitude towards equal temperament of English organists, that in 1879 William Pole, in his *Philosophy of Music*, should be writing:

> The modern practice of tuning all organs to equal temperament has been a fearful detriment to their quality of tone. Under the old tuning an organ made harmonious and attractive music, which was a pleasure to listen to. . . . Now, the harsh thirds, applied to the whole instrument indiscriminately, give it a cacophonous and repulsive effect.

A temperament which was considered to be good by C. P. E. Bach and other German musicians and theorists by the middle of the eighteenth century was still 'cacophonous and repulsive' to at least some English musicians at the end of the nineteenth. In such matters, England lagged behind other countries.

In 1511, Arnolt Schlick devised a temperament for each note of the chromatic scale. This is one of the earliest irregular temperaments, which, although it did not appear to have a strong influence on his contemporaries or successors, nor actually make the scale equally tempered, nevertheless did make possible the use of all keys, although some were less good than others. In the 1690s and the early years of the eighteenth century, many forms of tempering which allowed all keys to be used were being suggested by Werckmeister and Neidhardt. Both writers produced numerous different systems; a guide can do little more than point this out. J. Murray Barbour's comments on Neidhardt give some idea of the extent of the diversity in tempering; after discussing Neidhardt's work he writes:

> It will be of interest to consider which of his twenty systems Neidhardt considered the best. In the Sectio canonis he had said, "In my opinion, the first [of the circulating temperaments] is, for the most part, suitable for a village, the second for a town, the third for a city, and the fourth for the court." The fourth was equal temperament. . . .

In the following paragraph on the same page (page 179) in his book *Tuning and Temperament*, Murray Barbour writes:

> he then attempted to choose the best of these twenty tunings. He chose equal temperament, of course. . . .

Sectio canonis harmonici, from which Murray Barbour took his information, was published in 1724.

Another vote for equal temperament appears in the writings of C. P. E. Bach. In his *Essay on the True Art of Playing Keyboard Instruments*, published in 1753, he wrote:

> . . . . . . instruments must be tempered as follows; In tuning the fifths and fourths, testing minor and major thirds and chords, take away from most of the fifths a barely noticeable amount of their absolute purity.
>
> All twenty-four tonalities will thus become usable. . . . In practice, a keyboard so tuned is the purest of all instruments, for others may be purely tuned but they cannot be purely played. The keyboard plays equally in tune in all twenty-four tonalities. . . .

This brief outline, mentioning the practice in two countries only, helps to highlight the difficulties attendant upon any attempt to be precise about the tempering of keyboard instruments. It is very difficult to be sure, when so much diversity existed, what temperament would have been acceptable to any particular composer, In the *New Monthly Magazine* of 1 September 1811, James Broadwood proposed equal temperament, but was taken to task in his calculation of the size of perfect fifths by John Farey (Sn). James Broadwood replied that he was giving merely a practical method of producing equal temperament, 'its being in most general use, and because of the various systems it has been pronounced the best deserving that appellation by Haydn, Morzart and other masters of harmony'. James Broadwood gives no references to support his claim, but the movement towards equal temperament in the Germanic states seems to confirm his views. If so, his own company took another thirty-five years to accept a similar point of view, yet Mozart died in 1791 and Haydn in 1809. In England, Mozart's music would have been played on whatever temperament the instrument playing it happened to bear. It is possible that in the more fashionable concerts given by J. C. Bach and C. F. Abel the more up-to-date tempering was used, especially when one remembers that J. C. Bach was a student under the instruction of his elder brother C. P. E. Bach when the latter's *Essay*, which advocated equal temperament, was published. But did Mozart, on his visit to England in 1764, play on an equally tempered instrument? Did Haydn play on an equally tempered instrument when he visited London in 1791 and 1794? Who, at this time, can honestly answer these questions?

The 'who knows' type of argument can be carried too far. By using it, almost any temperament can be used for any music, if precise information is lacking. Certain facts do stand out as useful pointers, but the informed musician must be allowed to make decisions and given reasonable latitude in making them. From the writings of various theorists, meantone temperaments, which tend to keep the major thirds pure or nearly pure, were used for many years, at least from the fifteenth until the nineteenth centuries. Arnolt Schlick's lone but prophetic voice in 1511, advocating an irregular tempering to make all keys usable, had to remain unsupported until the late seventeenth century. Thereafter, the move to equal temperament in Germany appears to have been swift. Judging by the numerous writings opposed to it, equal temperament was making its presence felt in England at the beginning of the nineteenth century, but the spate of articles defending the key characteristics possible in an irregular temperament, did not hold it at bay entirely. In France, Mersenne seems, by an error, to have instituted a type of irregular tempering which persisted well into the eighteenth century. This error, according to Mark Lindley's article on temperament in *The New Grove* (1981), was 'due to the fact that Mersenne had not tuned a keyboard instrument himself' and therefore did not make it clear that, when tuning to ¼-comma meantone, fifths tuned upwards have their upper note flattened slightly, but fifths tuned downwards have their lower note sharpened slightly. For this reason, his instructions for tempering on the sharp side fit for ¼-comma meantone, but his instructions for tempering from F down to B flat, and from B flat down to E flat, seem to suggest that the lower note of these fifths was to be flattened, making them wide instead of narrow. This produced an irregular temperament which fitted the works of later composers better than pure ¼-comma.

Writings about temperament are inconclusive enough, but the music itself can, at times, be even less helpful. If a composition requires different notes from those which appear in the meantone scale described on page 48, it would appear that it should be played in an irregular, or in equal, temperament. Would that matters were as simple as that!

The first obstacle is re-tuning. If a composition requires D sharps but no E flats, it only takes a few minutes to convert all the E flats on a meantone tuned instrument into D sharps. Similarly, any other notes can be altered to give their enharmonic equivalents when both notes are not required.

A second obstacle is tolerance. Writings of many musicians testify that the inequalities inherent in the meantone system were tolerated. E flat could be used instead of D sharp and the resultant dissonance accepted as inevitable. Roger North, writing in the early eighteenth century, gives the following opinion:

> But since Musick for the most part is keyed upon the ordinary accords, it is best to hold them as perfect as may be, and not to corrupt them by sallving others seldome used. And there is less need because it is observed that the defects that will fall in the use of some keys, as F with a flat 3rd, natural B with a sharp third, and sharp F

with either sharp or flat third, and some others, by meer out-of-tunedness have certein caracters, very serviceable to the various purposes of Musick; as, to instance in one for all, F with a flat 3rd hath somewhat that more dolorous malencholy than any of the rest, and so others, in severall manners, well knowne to composers.

The chord 'F with a flat 3rd', or F minor, would, in meantone, be F, G sharp, C; a very dissonant sound. Roger North is not alone in his opinion. Charles Burney in *A General History Of Music* (1776–89) supports this view, even to mentioning the same key:

> It is somewhat remarkable that all the seven verse anthems which Dr. Boyce has inserted in his collection by the plaintive composer Pelham Humphrey, should by in flat keys; most of them in C and F minor, which are much out of tune on the organ by the usual temperament of that instrument; however, if well sung, these crude chords may add to the melancholy cast of the composition.

He is less sure of his ground when writing about the works of William Croft:

> ... the anthem for three voices from the eighty-eighth psalm is truly pathetic and expressive, from the beginning to the end; but unluckily, the key in which it is composed (F minor) is so much out of tune on the organ, as it is usually tempered, that the effect must be doubly offensive to those who, though possessed of good ears, are unable to account for it.

William Croft can, however, be considered as something of a special case, as will be explained later. The discrepancies caused by tempering were not only admitted, instructions were also given for minimising their effect.

Roger North's writings, that much worked mine of information, are quite specific on this point. The following appears as a footnote on page 155 of *Roger North on Music*, by John Wilson:

> 'Another use of the semitonian temperings' says North, 'is to abate the rancor of the scismes' on a keyboard instrument. . . . Thus, with the approximately Meantone Temperament advocated by North . . . the note tuned as G sharp is too flat to serve properly as A flat. But if it has to be so used, matters are improved 'by favoring the sharp G by a mixture with the note above (that is with natural A), be it by back-fall or slight trill' which will 'make the pipe or string sound as being a little sharper'. Similarly, if the available note is too sharp, it can be 'mixed' with the semitone below by means of a 'beat up or a slight trill'.

Much more could be written to support the notion among musicians of tolerance of the 'little dissonances' in instrumental music, as Christopher Simpson described them, but one further example, this time in musical notation, clinches the matter. In a *Fantasia* by Giles Farnaby, No 208 in the *Fitzwilliam Virginal Book* and No 9 in *Musica Britannica* Vol xxiv, the following passage, in modern edition appears;

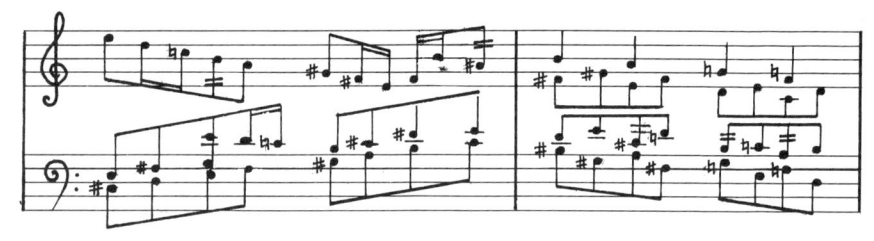

Example 9

In the original manuscript the passage was written as

Example 10

The notes are here written as they would have sounded, not D sharp and A sharp, but E flat and B flat, a fact which Richard Marlow's notes in *MB* Vol xxiv confirm. The dissonances caused by using these notes would have been accepted, and probably even enjoyed.

For all English keyboard music up to the end of the seventeenth century, and probably for much longer, including the famous Bull *Fantasia* (*MB* xiv No 17), a meantone temperament, probable ⅕-comma, suffices. Much has been made of the number of chromatic notes which appear in the *Fantasia*, and because of them a case has often been made for the use of equal temperament. In fact, it would almost certainly have been written for an instrument called a *clavicymbalum universale*, with a keyboard containing nineteen different notes within an octave. It had, in addition to the normal diatonic notes, C sharp and D flat, D sharp and E flat, F sharp and G flat, G sharp and A flat, A sharp and B flat, as well as separate keys for E flat and B flat. The addition of split keys to give alternative notes was one answer to tuning. The usual split keys were E flat and D sharp, G sharp and A flat, and possibly B flat and A sharp; the *clavicymbalum universale* was unusual in having so many split keys. The practice of using split keys did not meet with approval from musicians, and therefore died out after a fairly short period of time, although a square piano made by Zumpe, a German instrument maker who came to live and work in England in 1760, had eighteen different notes within an octave. This is a late date for split-keyed instruments because Roger North, as early as 1726 had written:

> Some experiments have bin made, by more additional pipes which they call Quarter Notes, to gain a perfection of the tune; but ever and besides the increase of charge and incumbrance in the fabrick (sufficient discouragement), they find it will not by any means be obtained to answer all the scales as may be required. Therefore the nicety is dropped and the masters are contented.

Robert Smith, on a similar subject, had written in 1749 that the expedient of 'inserting more keys in every octave is quite laid aside by reason of the difficulty of playing upon them', and Leopold Mozart, father of the famous Wolfgang Amadeus Mozart, confirmed that the practice had been discontinued in Germany by 1756.

Mersenne's error in describing the setting of ¼-comma meantone (see page 138) produced a temperament much used in France, but had an interesting influence on English music too. While studying English keyboard music of the late seventeenth and early eighteenth centuries, the author found that the music of William Croft presented most unusual problems in tempering. The music of all the other composers of the period could, with only a few moments of discomfort, be played on a standard meantone tuning, but the same could not be said for Croft. By experimenting with possible modifications to suit his music, it was found that it could be played on a temperament which accepted tuning in meantone fifths on the sharp side as far as G sharp, but in pure fifths on the flat side, C – F – B flat – E flat. The author had not then heard of the French temperament which does almost exactly that, except that the fifth C – F is still meantone and the F – B flat, and B flat – E flat fifths are slightly larger than true. Obviously Croft was taking advantage of a temperament which may well have come to England as part of the French influence in the wake of the restoration of the monarchy.

In the eighteenth century, discussion of temperament centres round *Das Wohltemperierte Clavier* of J. S. Bach. 'Well tempered' does not mean equal tempered, as has often been suggested. If a temperament was 'good' or an instrument 'well tempered', it could have been tuned in a number of different ways, one of which may have been equal temperament. It is most likely that the term referred to any form of tuning in which there was no particularly bad 'wolf' fifth; a tuning which, although it closed the gap in the circle of fifths allowing all keys to be used, still gave 'colour' to different keys by making some chords better than others. Had Bach intended equal temperament, he would have said so; as it is, a more convincing argument is that he was intending to demonstrate the characteristics of keys which, although usable, were in fact different.

The real meaning of differing qualities or characteristics of keys is difficult for anyone who has only heard equal temperament to understand. It is not, as might be expected, the same as the feelings generated by G major as compared with D flat major in Romantic music, where the one is bright and cheerful and the other warm and mellow. The warmth and mellowness disappear completely from D flat major in a meantone temperament, because it would be badly out of tune. It may, as Roger North puts it, have 'somewhat that more resembles a dolorous melancholy', but warmth and mellowness would have turned to a certain harshness. In an irregular temperament like those of Werckmeister, or the Vallotti or Thomas Young No 2, however, warmth and mellowness would have gently dissolved into a sort of faded quaintness due to the faster, but not unacceptable, beating of the mistuned intervals. Words are insufficient to describe the effect, the temperaments must be tried to be appreciated.

The key chord itself does not tell the complete story so far as key characteristics are concerned. The near relations in keys, in the form of dominant, subdominant and relative major and minor, also contribute to the general characteristics of the key. The greater the number of sharps and flats in the original key signature, the more likely its relatives are to be numbered among the poor chords, although in sharp keys the subdominant will always have one less sharp than the tonic, making movement to the flat side more in tune than movement on the sharp side, and the opposite is true of the flat keys.

Most irregular tunings contain pure as well as tempered fifths, and are therefore more directly Pythagorean in origin. One of the most interesting combinations is to have six pure and six tempered fifths. To close the circle of fifths combined with octaves, the six fifths would each have to be tempered by ⅙ of a Pythagorean comma (ie, by 4 cents). This form of tempering was advocated by F. A. Vallotti, who was Maestro di Capella of San Antonio, Padua, from 1728 until his death in 1780. It was also suggested by Thomas Young (1801), although his choice of pure fifths differs from that of Vallotti, and could also have been the ⅙-comma temperament of Gottfried Silberman, if the comma he intended happened to be the Pythagorean and not the syntonic. J. Murray Barbour in *Tuning and Temperament* calls the Thomas Young No 2 temperament 'the tuning of the "Out-of-Tune" piano, the sort of tuning into which a piano originally in equal temperament might fall if played upon by a beginner'. This is hardly a fair description of a beautifully subtle form of tempering, which, at the time of writing his description of it, Murray Barbour seems not to have heard. Instructions are given in the appendix for setting this temperament – it is well worth trying.

Erring on the side of opinions expressed by British writers in this whistle-stop tour through various regions of keyboard tempering has not been fortuitous. Most modern books which mention temperament tend to give prominence to German, French and Italian writers, and it would be an error to suppose that British opinion and practice ran parallel with that in other countries. The word 'British' is used advisedly, since many of the writers were of Scottish origin or published in Scotland. The ideas of the well-known Continental writers on temperament are easy to find, even though their writings are not always fully or accurately reported. It is less easy to find the opinions of British writers, who, although they did not lead the world in the moves towards equal temperament, helped, by their stubborn conservatism, to preserve variety in tuning almost long enough to see interest in it rekindled.

APPENDICES

1 Schemes for setting a variety of keyboard temperaments, with some notes on their use

General instructions for setting the temperaments
1 The notes from which to tune are shown as semibreves 𝅝 , the notes to be tuned are shown as crotchets without a stem ♩.
2 All checks are shown as two minims joined by a tail 𝅗𝅥𝅗𝅥.
3 The notes in brackets are those on which to focus attention when counting beats.
4 Tune all octaves true.
5 Tune all fifths true at first, a plus sign in the stave means that the INTERVAL is to be made greater than true.
6 Tune all fourths true at first, most of them will need to be made greater than true, but this will be shown in the scheme as a plus sign.
7 Do not forget that an interval can be made greater than true by sharpening the upper note or FLATTENING the lower note, and an interval can be made narrower than true by flattening the upper note or SHARPENING the lower.
8 Special instructions are given with some of the temperaments, more often than not, however, they simply remind, and reinforce the instructions given here.
9 The figures above and below the stave refer to the metronome settings required to give the beat rate for the intervals to be tuned or checked. Those above the stave are for standard pitch – c' 261.62 Hertz – while those below the stave are for low pitch – c' 246.76 Hertz.

¼-comma meantone
The chords of B, C sharp, F sharp and A flat major, and, F, A flat, B flat and E flat minor are poor, all other chords are good – much better than in equal temperament. There is no true chromatic scale because the 'semitones' vary in size, being a chromatic or a diatonic semitone depending on their relationship to the adjacent notes.
   The temperament is suitable for much early music, especially that in which the poorer chords do not need to feature prominently. It was most probably used from the early sixteenth century onwards. The general effect, compared with equal temperament, is 'stillness' which

¼-COMMA MEANTONE TUNING SCHEME

STAGE 1

All tuned fifths are narrow. All tuned fourths are wide. The figures above and below the stave are metronome settings for c' 261.62 and c' 246.76 respectively

¼-COMMA MEANTONE WITH SHARP G♯ TUNING SCHEME

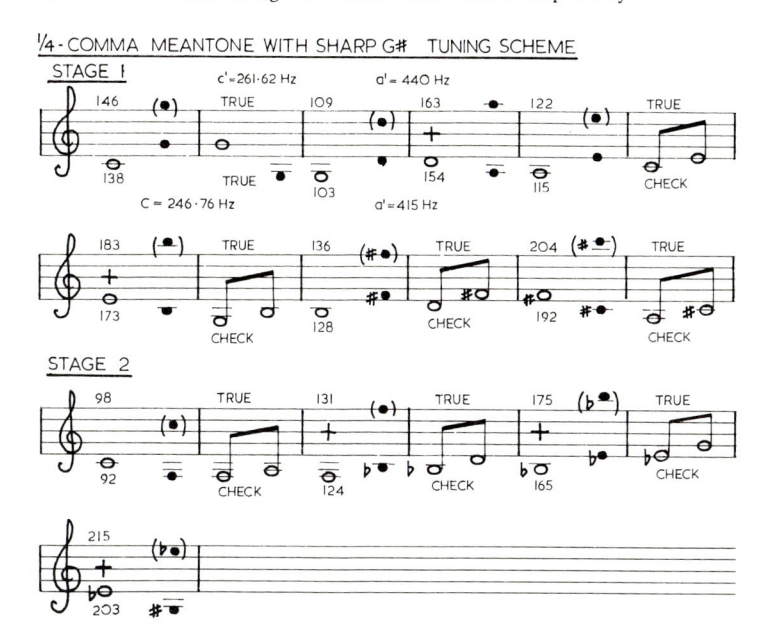

STAGE 1

STAGE 2

All tuned fifths are narrow except the last one in stage 2: $e'b - g\sharp$, which is wide. All tuned fourths are wide. The $e'b - g$ fifth should be tuned at twice a metronome speed of 107

can be in strong contrast to the occasional use of one of the out of tune chords.

¼-comma with a sharpened G sharp has similar characteristics except that E major and C sharp minor join the list of poor chords although they are tolerable, but in exchange there is a considerable improvement in the chords of A flat major and F minor. The chromatic scale is even worse as there is yet another size of 'semitone' introduced between the new G sharp and its immediate neighbours, G and A. There is documentary evidence reaching as far as the nineteenth century to support the suggestion that at least some tuners used the expedient of sharpening the G sharp so that it could roughly serve as both G sharp and A flat.

⅕-COMMA MEANTONE TUNING SCHEME

STAGE 1

STAGE 2

All tuned fifths are narrow. All tuned fourths are wide

⅕-comma meantone
Like ¼-comma, the chords of B, C sharp, F sharp and A flat major, and F, A flat, B flat and E flat minor, are poor, but they are all better than in ¼-comma. This benefit is gained at the expense of all the other major and minor chords which are slightly worse than in ¼-comma, but still better than in equal temperament. It is most likely that this rather than ¼-comma was the most used meantone temperament. This is certainly

APPENDICES

true of England and may well have been true of other European countries too. It is a suitable temperament for much of the early music repertory and was one of the temperaments in common use in England even as late as the beginning of the nineteenth century.

Since all the major thirds are slightly wide, they beat, whereas those of ¼-comma do not. This slight amount of beating adds an excitement which ¼-comma lacks.

⅕-comma with a sharp G sharp has similar advantages and disadvantages to the sharpening of the G sharp in ¼-comma. It may well have been the temperament used by some of the tuners employed by John Broadwood & Son in the early nineteenth century.

⅕-COMMA MEANTONE WITH SHARP G♯ TUNING SCHEME

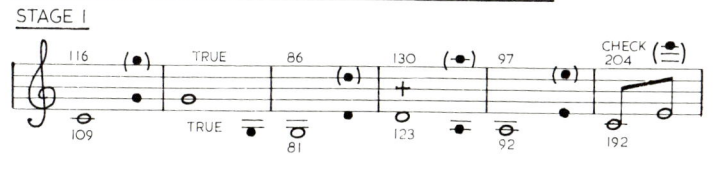

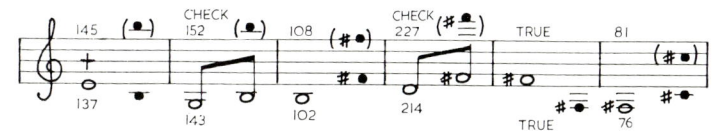

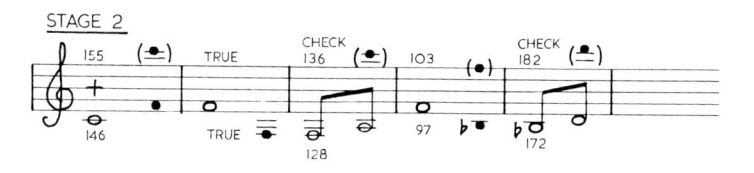

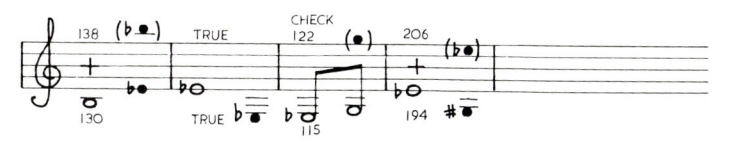

STAGE 1

STAGE 2

All tuned fifths are narrow, except last one in stage 2: $e'b - g\sharp$, which is wide. All tuned fourths are wide

⅕-COMMA MEANTONE (HAWKES MODIFICATION)

STAGE 1

STAGE 2

All tuned fifths are narrow. All tuned fourths are wide, apart from the two marked true

Hawkes' Modified ⅕-comma Temperament
This modified version of standard ⅕-comma meantone was advocated by William Hawkes as late as 1805 in his *Theory of Music*, and by the writer of an anonymous pamphlet entitled *A Treatise on the Theory and Practical System of Music* in 1798. It is not inconceivable that the pamphlet was also written by Hawkes.

The four poor major and minor chords associated with meantone temperaments remain, but there is an improvement in some of them when compared with unmodified ⅕-comma meantone. The improvements show mainly in the chord of A flat major and three of the four minor chords. The other chords are similar to those of unmodified ⅕-comma except for C minor which is not quite so good and C sharp minor which is considerably better.

FRENCH TEMPERAMENT

All tuned fifths are narrow, except $bb - f'$ which is wide. All tuned fourths are wide, except $bb - e'b$ which is narrow and $c'\sharp - g\sharp$ which is true

French Temperament

This temperament allows all chords to be used but those with few sharps and flats are, in general, better than those with many. The poorer chords of meantone are greatly improved, and since chords vary in quality, key characteristics are possible. This must be the correct temperament for late seventeenth- and early eighteenth-century French music, but there is evidence that it was also a fashionable newcomer on the English scene near the turn of the eighteenth century. (See chapter on the history of temperament and my article 'A Question of Temperament: Purcell and Croft' in the *Musical Times* of June 1978.)

THE VALLOTTI TEMPERAMENT

The tuned fifths $c' - g'$, $g - d'$ and $a - e'$ are narrow; the rest are true. The tuned fourths $d' - a$ and $e' - b$ are wide; the rest are true. Metronome figures above 208 should be divided by two or three and the appropriate number of beats counted for each swing

THOMAS YOUNG TEMPERAMENT No 2

The tuned fifths $c' - g'$, $g - d'$, $a - e'$ and $b' - f'\sharp$ are narrow; the rest are true. The tuned fourths $d' - a$ and $e' - b$ are wide; the rest are true

The Vallotti Temperament and Thomas Young No 2

These two temperaments are almost identical with six of their fifths tempered by ⅙ of a Pythagorean comma and the other six pure. The number of pure fifths makes them quick and easy to set. The only difference between them is in the positioning of the fifths.

Vallotti died in 1780 at the age of eighty-three, having spent most of his working life in Padua. Thomas Young published his method of tempering in the *Philosophical Transactions* of 1800. It is tempting to suggest that the Vallotti temperament found its way into England and was used there before 1800, but this is pure speculation; Thomas Young may well have reached his conclusions quite independently.

It is possible to play in any key using either of these temperaments and they each have four main 'colours' in major and minor keys. The best keys are akin to the better keys of ⅙-comma meantone and the poorest are very little worse than equal temperament. None of these colours is dull and lifeless, and the poorest of them add a touch of harmonic spice which is a delight. Their period suggests that they are suitable for middle and late eighteenth-century music, but their subtle colourations also make them equally attractive for much late classical and early romantic music.

The Werckmeister Temperaments 1 and 3

The two temperaments described here are numbered as they appear in *Tuning and Temperament* by J. Murray Barbour, although the numberings, as they appear in *Harpsichord Tuning* by G. C. Klop, and in *Fundamentals of Musical Acoustics* by A. H. Benade, are reversed. Further research is obviously needed to clarify the situation. Their publication date of 1691 must make them among the earliest of the irregular temperaments, and certainly among the first to receive a wide circulation. Correct Temperament No 1, as it appears here, is the most famous of Werckmeister's many temperings, and the better of the two described here. Its worst chord is C minor, and its best are F major and A minor. Apart from its best and poorest chords, it closely resembles the Vallotti and Thomas Young No 2 temperaments for quality. All keys are usable, even C minor, and there is a variety of key colour. In No 3, key colour is also possible, but its poorest chords are appreciably worse than those of No 1, and F minor is scarcely tolerable.

Werckmeister temperaments, especially No 1, are well suited to the music of Bach and Handel and probably closely resemble the type of tempering which Bach himself preferred; the poor C and F minor chords are a disadvantage rather than a disaster.

WERCKMEISTER CORRECT TEMPERAMENT No 1

Fifths $c' - g'$, $g - d'$ and $b - f\sharp$, are narrow; the rest are pure. The fourth $d' - a$ is wide; the rest are pure

WERCKMEISTER CORRECT TEMPERAMENT No 3

Fifths $a - e'$ and $f\sharp - c'\sharp$ are narrow and $g\sharp - e'b$ is wide; the rest are true. The fourths $d' - a$ and $c'\sharp - g\sharp$ are wide, the other tuned fourths are pure

EQUAL TEMPERAMENT

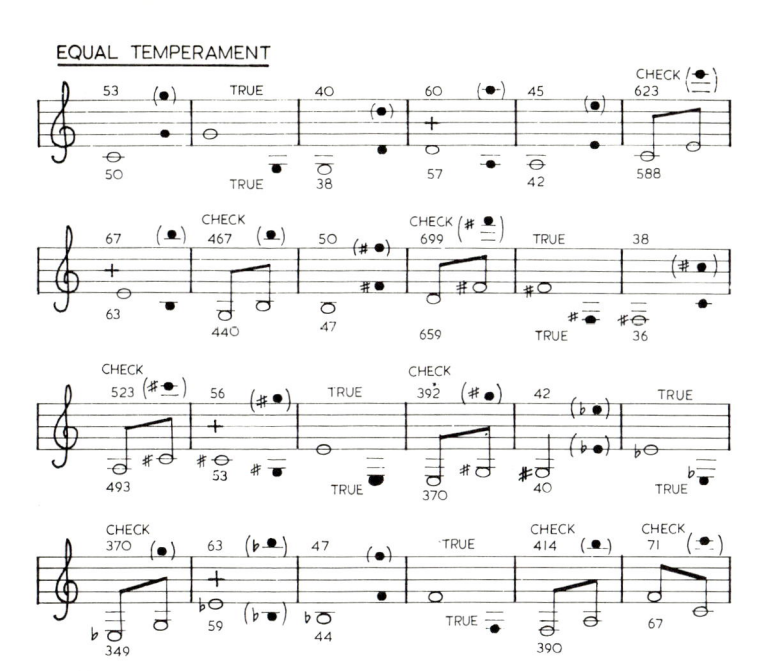

All fifths are narrow. All fourths are wide. Metronome figures below 60 should be doubled and the beat rate taken from each alternate swing of the metronome. Figures above 208 should be divided by two or three and the appropriate number of beats should be counted for each swing, eg $f - a = 414 \div 3 = 138$. Set metronome to 138 and count three beats for every swing of the metronome

Equal Temperament

Because of its fashionability, equal temperament is considered to be suitable for keyboard music of any period. This is, to say the least, questionable. It is a comparative new-comer on the scene and fulfils the requirements of keyboard music from the mid- to late eighteenth-century onwards, although there must be grave doubts about its authenticity in many places before the early, or even the mid-nineteenth century. Its great advantage is that it allows for unlimited modulation, and, in the twentieth century, has even been used as an absolute scale by serial composers. Its use in this way must be suspect, since it is highly unlikely that even on a well-tuned piano, exact equality is established, and it must be a certainty that it never is on instruments which are free to alter pitch at will. The impossibility of such equality was shown by Llewellyn S. Lloyd, the eminent writer on acoustics and temperament, as long ago as 1940, in his excellent article in *Music and Letters* entitled 'The Myth of Equal Temperament'.

Having said all this, it does remain as a useful compromise for a keyboard, or more correctly, for a piano. During the later history of the organ, it is also acceptable (with great reluctance in England), but for harpsichords and the like, except for a short period during that instrument's decline in the late eighteenth century, it is only really suitable for music written during the twentieth century.

2 Table giving the cent value of a variety of intervals within an octave

Cents	Description of interval
2	Schisma: the interval by which eight 5ths plus a major 3rd exceeds five octaves
22	Syntonic Comma, or comma of Didymus; the interval by which four pure fifths exceed two octaves and a pure major third
24	Ditonic Comma, or comma of Pythagoras; the interval by which twelve pure fifths exceed seven octaves
42	Diesis; the interval by which an octave exceeds three pure major thirds
76	¼-comma meantone chromatic semitone
100	Equally tempered semitone
112	Diatonic semitone of the pure scale
117	¼-comma meantone diatonic semitone
193	¼-comma meantone full tone
200	Equally tempered full tone
204	Full tone in the pure scale
294	Pythagorean minor third
300	Equally tempered minor third
310	¼-comma meantone minor third
316	Pure minor third
386	Pure major third
400	Equally tempered major third
408	Pythagorean major third
498	Pure perfect fourth
500	Equally tempered perfect fourth
503	¼-comma meantone perfect fourth
600	Equally tempered augmented fourth/diminished fifth
610	Pure diminished fifth
697	¼-comma meantone perfect fifth
700	Equally tempered perfect fifth
702	Pure perfect fifth
772	¼-comma meantone augmented fifth
800	Equally tempered augmented fifth/minor sixth
814	Pure minor sixth
884	Pure major sixth
890	¼-comma meantone major sixth
900	Equally tempered major sixth
996	Pure minor seventh
1000	Equally tempered minor seventh
1007	¼-comma meantone minor seventh
1083	¼-comma meantone major seventh
1088	Pure major seventh
1100	Equally tempered major seventh
1110	Pythagorean major seventh
1200	Octave

GLOSSARY

Cent The unit used for measuring intervals – equal to the hundredth part of an equally tempered semitone
Circulating temperament A temperament in which all keys are usable, but some are more in tune than others
Comma The name given to some of the discrepancies which arise when trying to fit together pure intervals in series
  Syntonic Comma The interval by which four pure fifths exceed two octaves and a major third – 22 (or more exactly 21.506281) cents
  Pythagorean Comma The interval by which twelve pure fifths exceed seven octaves – 24 (or more exactly 23.459894) cents
Diesis The interval by which an octave exceeds three pure major thirds – 42 (or more exactly 41.05903) cents
Discord A chord which requires resolution
Dissonance An interval in which beats are produced by the two notes themselves or by their harmonics
Enharmonic A change of note name but not of pitch – eg C sharp/D flat
Frequency Rate of recurrence of vibrations; measured in Hertz; 440 vibrations per second equal 440 Hertz
Irregular temperament A system of tuning in which the tuning intervals (fifths and fourths) vary in size
Just Pure
Just Intonation A form of tuning based on the pure octave, pure fifth and pure major third
Pure interval An interval in which there are no beats between the notes or their harmonics
Pythagorean tuning A tuning system based on the pure fifth and the pure octave
Regular temperament A system of tuning in which all the fifths and fourths used in tuning remain constant
Schisma The difference between the ditonic and syntonic commas, 2 (or more exactly 1.9536325) cents
Split key Separate keys, or a single key divided, to give enharmonic equivalents, eg one key divided across the middle giving D sharp when one half is pressed and E flat when the other is pressed
Wolf A dissonant interval produced in the process of tuning, eg the apparent 'fifth' G sharp – E flat in a meantone temperament which is very much out of tune

BIBLIOGRAPHY

Apel, Willi *The Harvard Dictionary of Music* (Heinemann, 1970)
Bach, C. P. E. *Essay on the True Art of Playing Keybord Instruments* (Berlin, 1753; trans W. J. Mitchell, Eulenburg, 1974)
Backus, J. *The Acoustical Foundations of Music* (John Murray, 1969)
Baines, F. *A Tutor for the Treble Viol* (Gamut, 1973)
Barbour, J. M. *Tuning and Temperament* (Michigan State College Press, 1951; reprinted Da Capo, 1972)
Bartholomew, W. T. *Acoustics of Music* (Prentice Hall, 1942)
Bellow, A. *Illustrated History of the Guitar* (New York, 1970)
Benade, A. H. *Fundamentals of Musical Acoustics* (OUP, 1976)
Blades, J. *Orchestral Percussion Technique* (OUP, 1973)
Blades, J. *Percussion Instruments and their History* (Faber, 1970)
Bottrigari, E. *Il Desiderio* (1594; trans McClintock, American Institute of Musicology, 1962)
Boyden, D. D. *The History of Violin Playing* (OUP, 1965)
Brinsmead, E. *History of the Pianoforte* (London, 1879)
Broadwood, H. F. *Some Notes made by J. S. Broadwood 1838, with observations and Elucidations by H. F. Broadwood* (London, 1862)
Burney, C. *A General History of Music* (London, 1776, 1782 and 1789; reprinted Dover, 1957)
Carse, A. *Musical Wind Instruments* (MacMillan, 1939; reprinted, Da Capo, 1965)
Clementi, M. *The Art of Playing the Pianoforte* (London, 1801; reprinted, Da Capo, 1974)
Cowling, E. *The Cello* (Batsford, 1975)
Dolmetsch, N. *Twelve Lessons on the Viola da Gamba* (Schott, 1950)
Donington, R. *Instruments of Music* (Methuen, 1949; 3rd edition, 1970)
Donington, R. *Interpretation of Early Music* (Faber, 1974)
Elgar, R. *Introduction to the Double Bass* (Published privately, 1960; reprinted, 1969)
Elgar, R. *More About the Double Bass* (Published privately, 1963; reprinted 1969)
Elgar, R. *Looking at the Double Bass* (Published privately, 1967)
Fischer, J. C. *Piano Tuning, a Simple and Accurate Method for Amateurs* (Baker, 1907; reprinted, 1975)
Galpin, F. W. *Old English Instruments of Music* (Methuen 1910; 4th edition, 1965)
Gregory, R. *The Horn, A Guide to the Modern Instrument* (Faber, 1961)

BIBLIOGRAPHY

Hayes, G. R. *Musical Instruments and their Music*, Vol 2. (OUP, 1930)
Helmholtz, H. *On the Sensations of Tone* Trans A. J. Ellis (1885; reprint, Dover, 1974)
Heron-Allen, E. *Violin making; as it was, and is* (Ward Lock, 1885)
Howe, A. H. *Scientific Piano Tuning and Servicing* (New York, 1941; reprint of 3rd edition, 1966)
Hubbard, F. *Three Centuries of Harpsichord Making* (Harvard University Press, 1965)
Jorgensen, O. *Tuning the Historic Temperaments by Ear* (North Michigan University Press, 1977)
Klop, G. C. *Harpsichord Tuning Course Outline* (Garderen, Holland, 1974)
Lindley, M. 'Early Sixteenth Century Keyboard Temperaments' *Musica Disciplina* Vol xxviii, 1974, pp129–51
Lindley, M. 'Instructions for the Clavier Diversly Tempered' *Early Music* Vol 5 No 1 January 1977
Liston, H. *An Essay upon Perfect Intonation* (Edinburgh, 1812)
Lloyd, L. S. *Intervals, Scales and Temperaments* (Macdonald & Jame's, 1963)
McCombie, I. *The Piano Handbook* (David & Charles, 1980)
Meffen, J. 'A Question of Temperament: Purcell and Croft' *Musical Times* June 1978
Mersenne, M. *Harmonie Universelle* (Paris, 1635)
Monkemeyer, H. *Method for the Bass Viol* (Moeck, Celle, 1959)
Mozart, L. *A Treatise on the Fundamental Principles of Violin Playing* (Augsburg, 1759; trans Knocker, OUP, 1948)
Nelson, S. M. *The Violin and Viola* (Ernest Benn, 1972)
North, R. *Memories of Music* (Ed E. F. Rimbault, London, 1846)
Playford, J. *An Introduction to the Skill of Musick* (London, 1674; facsimile edition, Gregg, 1966)
Pole, W. *The Philosophy of Music* (London, 1879)
Quantz, J. J. *On Playing the Flute* (Berlin, 1752; trans Reilly, Faber, 1966)
Remnant, M. *Musical Instruments of the West* (Batsford, 1978)
Russell, R. *The Harpsichord and Clavichord* (Faber, 1973)
Sachs, C. *History of Musical Instruments* (Dent, 1942)
Sadie, Dr Stanley. *The New Grove* (Macmillan, 1981)
Scholes, P. A. *The Oxford Companion to Music* (London, 1938; reprinted OUP, 1970)
Simpson, C. *The Division Viol* (London, 1659; reprint of 1667 edition, Curwen, 1965)
Smith, E. *Pianos in Practice* (Scolar Press, 1978)
Stevens, F. A. *Piano Tuning, Repair and Rebuilding* (Nelson Hall, 1972)
Taylor, C. A. *The Physics of Musical Sounds* (English Universities Press, 1965)

Turnbull, H. *The Guitar from the Renaissance to the Present Day* (Batsford, 1974)

Van der Straeton, E. S. J. *History of the Violoncello* William Reeves (London, 1914; reprinted 1971)

Wilson, J. (Ed) *Roger North on Music* (Novello, 1959)

Young, T. 'Outline of Experiments and Inquiries Respecting Sound and Light' *Philosophical Transactions* Vol xc (1800) pp106-50

INDEX

banjo, 128
bass bar, 114
bearings, laying the, 75ff
beating, 22-3, 35-7, 38-9, 41ff, 57-8, 77ff, 92
beats, how to calculate, 47-8
beats, how to listen for, 23-5
brass instruments, tuning, 91-2
bridge, 65, 116
bridge, height of, 119
bugle, 100

cents, 19-20, 30ff, 35ff, 40-9, 71-2
clarinet, 102-3
clavichord, 9, 39, 65, 87-8, 132
comma, ditonic, 21, 36-8, 56, 75
comma, syntonic, 21, 36-7, 56, 71
concert pitch, 12
Cooper's scale, 105
crook, 100-1

Didymus, comma of, 21, 36-7, 56, 71
diesis, 21
difference tone, 27-9
double bass, 120

edge tone, 103
enharmonic, 20
equal temperament, 9, 29, 36-7, 40ff, 59ff, 70-1, 74, 77ff, 89, 93, 118, 122, 132-3, 153

finger holes, 10, 11, 34
flute, 102, 105
French temperament, the, 149
frequency, 27-8, 40ff
frets, 11, 110, 121
fretted instruments, 9, 34, 110-12, 121ff

guitar, 5-6, 8-9, 34, 126-7

hammer technique, 68ff
hammer, tuning, 66, 83
harmonic series, 18, 23
harmonics, 18-19, 22, 27, 39ff
harmonics, training to listen for, 24ff
harp, 11, 34, 132
harpsichord, 39, 46, 65, 85-6
hitch pin, 65
horn, 100

keyboard instruments, 9, 35, 39, 62-3, 64ff

keyboard tuning, 64ff, 70ff, 83ff
key colour, 142

laying the bearings, 75ff
lute, 127

mandolin(e), 128
meantone, 36-8, 42-3, 47, 59, 71ff, 74-5, 82, 86, 133-4, 144-8
meantone, calculations for, 50-2
meantone chords, 73ff

nut, 64-5, 87, 112-14, 125

oboe, 102-3
overblow, 96

Papps wedge, 83
pegs, 115
percussion instruments, 129ff
piano, 10, 20, 23, 34, 65, 82-5
pin, hitch, 65
pin, wrest, 64ff, 85-6
pitch, 9, 12-14, 26
pitch, concert, 12
pitch for early instruments, 13
pitch memory, 57ff
pitch, standard, 13, 91
pitch variation, hearing, 19-20
pure intervals, 25ff
pure scale, 30-3
Pythagorean comma, 21, 36-7, 71, 75
Pythagorean scale, 36-7
Pythagorean tuning, 133

rebec, 120
recorder, 10, 28, 102, 106-8
reed instruments, 103
retuning, 138
'rule of the eighteenth', 127

saxophone, 102
scale, chromatic, 17, 36
scale, diatonic, 17, 29
scale, meantone, 36-8
scale, pure, 30-3
scale, setting a, 76ff
schisma, 21
scordatura, 111
series, harmonic, 18, 23
setting a scale, 76ff
'setting up' a stringed instrument, 115-16

INDEX

sound-board, 64-5
sound-post, 114-16
spinet, 39, 65, 87, 132
stringed instruments, tuning of, 109ff, 116ff
strings, preventing the breaking of, 67
strings, replacing, 114
temperament, 39-40, 67, 89-90
temperament, equal, 9, 36-7, 40ff, 70-1, 74ff, 93, 118, 122, 132-3
temperament, French, 149
temperament, history of, 132ff
temperament, irregular, 74ff, 82, 86, 133
temperament, the need for, 16ff
temperament versus tuning, 7-12
tempering, 21, 33-63
tempering a major 3rd, 45-6
tempering a major 6th, 46-8
tempering a perfect 5th, 39-43
tempering a perfect 4th, 44-5
timpani, 129, 131
tone meter, 53
tones, greater and lesser, 31ff
trombone, 10, 91-2, 100
tuning, 6, 7-12, 52-3
tuning fork, 83
tuning hammer, 66, 83, 85
tuning hammer technique, 68ff
tuning key, 83-5
tuning a clavichord, 87
tuning a harpsichord, 85
tuning keyboards, 70ff
tuning a piano, 83-4
tuning a spinet, 87
tuning stringed instruments, 109ff, 116ff
tuning a virginals, 86
tuning in performance, 54-63
tuning, Pythagorean, 133
tuning versus temperament, 7-12
tuning, what is, 5-7

ukalele, 128

valve, 10-11, 34, 96-100
vibrato, 62, 125
viola, 9, 56-7
violin, 5, 7-9, 53-5, 109, 118-9
violin family, 112ff
violoncello, 9, 119
viols, 9, 34, 121, 123-4
viols, tuning, 123
virginals, 39, 65, 86-7, 132

wedge, 76-7, 83
Wohltemperierte Clavier, Das, 142
'wolf' intervals, 38, 72ff, 142
woodwind instruments, 13-14, 101ff
woodwind instruments, tuning, 91
wrest pins, 64ff, 68-9, 84-5
wrest plank, 64ff